Day Trading 101: How To Day Trade Stocks For Passive Income

SADANAND PUJARI

Published by SADANAND PUJARI, 2024.

Table of Contents

Copyright 1

About 2

What is Forex Day Trading? 3

Forex Trading Details 5

Lot Sizes and PiPs 8

EURUSD 1h Day Trading 10

EURUSD 30M Day Trading 20

EURUSD 5M Day Trading 28

USDCHF 1h Day Trading 37

USDCHF 30M Day Trading 45

USDCHF 5M Day Trading 54

USDJPY 1H Day Trading 64

USDJPY 30M Trading - Risk Management 73

USDJPY 5M Day Trading 82

What is Short Selling? 91

Short Sale Metrics 94

Sources of short interest data 99

What is Fibonacci Retracement? 102

Fibonacci Retracement in Detail 103

Demo Account 112

VIX 114

Support, Resistance & Trendlines 123

Copyright

Copyright © 2024 by **SADANAND PUJARI**

All rights reserved. No part of this book may be reproduced, scanned, or distributed in any printed or electronic form without permission. Please do not participate in or encourage piracy of copyrighted materials in violation of the author's rights. Purchase only authorized editions.

Day Trading 101: How To Day Trade Stocks For Passive Income

Learn The Basics Of Stock Market Day Trading: Chart Setting, Technical Patterns, Indicators, Gappers & Breakaway Runners

First Edition: Jun 2024

Book Design by **SADANAND PUJARI**

About

Day Trading 101: Learn How To Day Trade for Profit is a Book designed to teach you the visual power of price/volume spikes and drops occurring during consolidations and breakout patterns.

This Book will teach you how to take advantage of potential price/volume activity before large price movements appear on the chart.

Take this Book now and learn from my 10+ years of experience. Avoid the most common pitfalls that catch 90% of traders!

Too often beginner traders enter the market without the necessary knowledge and practice needed. As a result they take excessive, expensive and unnecessary risks hoping for higher returns. This Book will teach you a very effective way to trade in the market successfully and with confidence.

This Book is for all levels: beginners, intermediate and advanced traders! All you need is an open mind and a passion to be successful!

Enroll in this Book now and start trading the market successfully!

What is Forex Day Trading?

What is for next day tricky Florac creating means buying and telling them the same day trading basically for exchange trading is used to remove the need to pay fees for holding position or whatnot as some brokers charge for it. And usually the child is so high that your profitability can't get reduced whereas in foreign exchange trading those fees don't apply. So you can easily make money and expect Day trading is a highly speculative trading activity. However they are important part of market because they are the one that hold the market intact because if there is so much selling and there are no day traders then there would be no lifeline between the gateway because everyone knew that there wouldn't be a buyer that as good as the one who jumps in buys and sells at a higher rate and Except so people can see higher and lower prices on the same day helping them create stakeholder is misunderstood by many traders and I use the term it is misunderstood.

But Ortega's example is not a get rich quick scheme. You have to remember it is not get rich quick scheme turning names many great with lots of money for brokers because they are earning commissions and in many cases you will be like few saints and there will be one or two that will be in good dot.com raked $10 $4 or like in good presentation. So today as many trades you will have a good profit in your account but you have to make many many tricks and you have to sit right in front of the market are you going to do anything. So you have to invest time and money only because you have to be prepared before the day's trading. Your broker will be making easy money so he will be happier but you as an investor will be making far up. However it's not a quick screen. You will be earning smaller amounts every day and in the long run they will be a good mark. But I repeat I'm seeing the long run.

Forex Trading Details

Phonics creating tales now for the market is a global market and the market itself. Tick-Tock Main Street or for experts. So there's no foreign government or player determining the rate of fire experts it calculated are set by the market. Becky spent themself to one who is buying would be putting up a price and have to sell it again. Then he will sell. And therefore it's a complete market no one controls it for its market is the second biggest market after the debt Okereke market. So it's one of the biggest markets. And in terms of his intention was to exceed one of the biggest because the debt of great market that he can investors are back mostly they are like far more active in forex market in terms of tech market major players in this market are the big banks and hedge funds because basically we have to be against buying or selling power.

As currencies I didn't post before. Dexys does not accept a value to them because it's one pair. Tell us daughter against could break pound S.N. pair usually means that one U.S. dollar is but one point one pound behind the scenes. Banks run firms known as D-don't help in trading. The danger is that it basically makes the market. They are the market makers. This trading market is quite an inter-bank pocket. The banks trade in between themselves and the dealers hoping for market help. International trade by showing an exchange rate so people would know that this is the exchange rate. If they were to buy a one U.S. dollar they would have to pay one point quickly and that's how it has to international trade because Douban is great.

6

No one will be able to sell or buy because they won't know what that thing is put in. But keeping the petrifies you have put your platoon's one currency by selling the other current that simply you're getting one currency in exchange for that currency. And that's how far a bear in Florida is. Margaret market formed in the 1970s under Purton word system innuendo's the exchange rate rates were fixed it was fixed that one you start will be based on one point one redbrick. But now almost all countries are based on floating exchange risk which means that democracy means right and it's not fixed and therefore you can easily make money for them.

Because it's not fixed at a fixed rate. It doesn't change. So no one controls the market and makes money. And before that is fixed in a floating exchange rate you could hear news that helps build a strong market and helps make easy money. Frank's market is the most liquid market in the world because every time someone is selling and buying. So there is liquidity in the market and bigger or smaller players can easily buy or sell flight's market works 24 hours a day for a day trader heaven. However, Flake's market first you are watching. So the return rate is far lower now. Many brokers offer higher leverage but I'm against them. I usually suggest you do have a hundred percent of your own money that is 20 , 30 or 40 percent of leverage.

So it means hanging 40 percent of the buying power. Now if you look for Fiat brokers they usually offer thousand times leverage as well which means a small move against you. Well wipe out your account with 10 seconds before and the day trader your first aim is to be in the market is to be a trader.

Therefore you don't take high leverage because at the end of the day money will come to your account automatically. My plan is so good. The question needs a high leverage and can wipe you out. So you have to trade in those which make you in the market and you should not be like stock now. The Forex market is a five point nine trillion market per day. And I'm using it as an average number. So on some days it's more than five point thirty nine trillion. So just look at the Matney Duke tax why it is so that he could market money making market and.

Lot Sizes and PiPs

Lot sizes and now historically far extruding was done in yutz Danberg Lauck is ten hundred thousand units. New York is 10000 unique and microlight is one thousand units. So basically when you are, you're putting your patches in locked and Unix which helps you understand how much money you make now to hire locks that couldn't make a good profit from an extremely smart move. Because higher units are like Target for 100000 unique even on a one pip you're making a hundred thousand pair profit only on a 1 1 Pay profit. Now what is up it means the smallest price change in forex trading. So it's like the lowest priced and the lowest it could be like in the dollar. You have the last hit. What kinks when tanked is the lowest CMB in forex trading. The first is one pip most for Express are priced a preferred decimal point.

That means 0.00 0 1 means one pip biffo the smallest gain for most for fixed rates is equal to one is 200 off 1 percent. As simple as that. So basically in Frakes you're not aiming for 1 percent you're aiming for one is 200 out of 1 percent. Now in Forex you have profits and you are shown in papers and Pipps is money to conclude the. You need to deduct the buying price from the selling price. Example If USD Frank was back at $1 2 1 5 5 cents and so that one down to 1 5 9 cents then it moved for PIP because if you remember I told you that you focus on four decimal points. That is zero point 0 0 0 1 so you deduct points. Also you one point 2 1 5 5 minus 1 point 2 1 5 9. That is the buying price first and selling price later. Zero point zero zero zero for which means for Pipp.

Now each country has its own value both for one purpose differing for each pair because it could be let's say ninety five 0.9 five. One takes the Byne rate and so on and so forth. So all prices are different. You just need to read the buying price from the selling price. Now the question comes up: What is your profit? Because at the end of the day the money in your pocket is what counts. The value of Pepper is calculated as Bap. You think when you do 1 divided by top ten thousand divided by exchange rate. Example U.S. dollar euro is trading at point seven do so in two and we one pick. So when people and to point 0 0 0 1 divided by the exchange rate 0.72 shown to and you'll get to on this point you know there are 0 1 teacakes. Now let's bring you back into the picture because basically you're buying and look now your profit was in 0 0 0 0 1 3 8.

You can simply apply a lock for example for Stardock you might apply 0.00 28 might be paperback 10000 units so you get our daughter and a techie or tent if you can pick up then just multiply 1.8 by 10. $13 and fence. So this is how the more people you get, the more profit you make and you're investing a lower amount. Now Japanese yen is an exception as it doesn't come in one divided by 10000. Putin comes in one divided by 100. So if you are happy the end is trading at one 2051 then to calculate one pip you need to decide 0.01 that one point 20 Darton 51 cents. Now tinctures are nowadays normal. So far I expect you to Whiting's $0.03 01. But in the end it could self-dual 0.01. So by dividing it you get down to zero point zero zero you know 0 8. You don't think so. Dax what dockside and pips are two.

EURUSD 1h Day Trading

Hi guys today you discuss girls you just don't appear on the 60 minute chart. You can see here it's one hour. You've selected the candlestick chart. That is the thing that counts sticks and the afflicted pulling up on an AM CD. Just to sum it up to top I'd a direct number is redlines number. For that we go beyond the top number is the topline number and the bottom number is to park in line. And for the MTD the blue line numbers here the red line number is here. And this is when it crosses up. So it will be a positive number if it crosses down. It will be a negative number. Now just to show you as I've discussed previously whenever you see double loads triple lows on the CD Remember you are in for a jackpot. Now as it crosses here you'll be buying and be ready to make a good amount.

Now one thing that I have learned from my students is that they want to know what to do in these kinds of circumstances where you buy right here at eight to a minute. Right here at one point one takes one two and you sell late. Too many. Yep right here at one point 1 5 8 9. So let me get a calculator out to show you the peps we bought here at one point 1:06 went to minus. We sold it here at one point 1 5 nine. So it's 20 pips right now. That's a huge loss for many traders. Now for them I first suggest they go for a shorter time period because the losses become shorter and they won't be having that kind of issue number one. Number two is if you do not like it, except this kind of last night Old-World brings up stopwatches, for example slow Denslow. If you check this out.

One point sixty three. This is an extremely Frausto for you but here you are no would have been below this red line. Let's say on dealer discount. But once it made the line go up then low below the dragline is an important reason if you got stuck stopping outcry not backtrack. Number one. Number two if the price gets stuck at your rate if you see the price getting stuck at your rate then let's get out. If you're crazy enough, leverage. I repeat if you created leverage because for a person who creates with his own money that's not a problem. But in fact keeps on excessive leverage. Then he should get out if the price is not following the MSEE because remember one is you're following the embassy to make sure that the price follows that and believe that the MSCP makes the price right now.

Now whenever it doesn't make the price that up run up and it goes straight that when you have to understand that it's something wrong. And as a leverage player you can not set into a forex peer or into a stock or into a commodity. Then there's something wrong because leverage is a commodity. So you have to understand that in the leverage and the price is not going up because if you look at it we brought it to twenty six seven eight nine ten. It's 10 hours and it's not doing anything. And after buying it if it would have gone somewhat up let's put him. Brought it here and it would have gone up and then went straight down. That was not a bad move. Then you could have placed yourself plus on this open so that you like kept him in position if it went down that's not packed because he won.

You know not stating Craig because not closing is not a good trade but forget stocks at your rate then that's a tricky point because the moment it goes down you've warned me that you are very concerned because there are lows on the bottom. So the rule number one is if you're in leverage and the price is not going to get out don't sit in it if you will it won't help you because leverage itself is costing you. So get out now and move further. And if I just how for you simply buy the crossover MSEE example right. Next 1.1 583. Let me play one point 1 5 8 3 right here. And then the price moves higher. See if Ruth moves works now. OK. Whenever the crossing was high.

Because you could look at it if you then checked this line that I'm just showing you it's about Picross on the up side. Now when you see this tricky moment because you're actually it will rise for me as I have done right now but if I look at the price it's not costing up because the fact that it will become a single thing about an on top and that would be the best thing ever because that would tell you that you are on the right track but it's not costing not a good moment in time so you wait. See that misleading term grossing up. But the price is not costing us now in that case I want to sell now and never sell Vache by the action stop loss. Now some of you might ask what actual stop loss actions topless Newnes let's. I'm putting up a discount. Gore countered.

Is our actions so grossly Blewett that is the time to take action. So remember this if it crosses below decks your time to take action. But if you look at the price, it is still going up. Now right here on this kind of income. So quiet after are you going to burn that up and Methodius moving down. If you make it big. Well it's disappointing. No. Never mind that it's going down. So if you sell here remember to get back in. But if you remember our price or like buying rate is here on this close one point twenty five 8:3. So we are not that much concerned to see the price move up and then go down, move up and then go down with us or RSA baby boom and is not getting crushed up. That tells you that and doubling the by now is the price of Grandcolas natural and bufo your point like your buying point is in a tech world situation.

If you just focus on it and the price doesn't go up above doubling up and then over remember the embassy is about to come down with a gap between the two lines one line and the red line narrows. That's when the crossover is happening. See crosshair happen now. If you would have a pocket here and he would hold on to close us discounting then you won't have made so much money. You bought a car and you're selling it here 1.1 Pif. Sorry. Here 1 1 5 8 6 5 minus one point twenty five six. You have made only a t Pip's profit now. That's not a good profit but if you remember I started telling you that today was a problem.

Timothy was crossing up but the price was not and as it was going straight to bring up I was contracting because no one in the bank was getting higher and higher pulling the bank was not going up. So the gap between them was shrinking and shrinking almost means not a good moment because if you're trading with the shrink you won't be able to make money. That's the normal rule of thumb. Now the point of view is that this plan that I'm discussing doesn't give you just the best point and still gives you at least a profit. Now if you have your break up you wait wait wait and wait to look at the price even falling as it's told remaining within doubling about that.

That's a good thing right. And a two minute collect me check 00 step into Yeah this is the buying point. At one point 1 5 9 at one point twenty five dollars. So you have to make when I can on this day and you're waiting body go slow one year I can't. So it's a solemn moment. At one point twenty five Blake minus one point twenty five eight eleven. Plus. Now you are in for a pimp and you lost that sound. Applause. Right. But this is part of the game as I always tell my student please please please don't take a bad moment but don't take excessive leverage. If you ask me what's the leverage I will donate 130 percent 140 percent but not above it by hiring 40 percent. I mean 100 percent of your own money and percent of the leverage. Or 40 percent of leverage but 40 percent is excessive. It's like just the boundaries of excessive leverage.

Now if you really care right now wait wait wait. Now if you focus on the feeding you will see what you will see as you're seeing your pillows on a. Was not breaking to tell so the same thing is happening right. So tell us it's OK. It's not that bad. See it's costing up to buying on and up right. And if you remember we make a profit here and we lose pay for proper care. So it's a loss. Now I am buying it again at one point, one 2:54 right. Now once you have bought it the price jumps outside the building of an daks. First of all a good move although after that you are seeing it coming back on track for a long time. If you look at it it's not crossing up. This is the third time I remember. And this is a night to remember. So it's like days because it's an hour long chalk. It's a long period of time.

It does fall off back to anything not crossing down. So much higher and higher it does fall off again but moves higher and higher. Just look at it now. Right now it's getting like going inside the polling. And but you all like toppling the band while still pointing up, which is a good thing. But you're pointing lower back down. That's not a good thing. But you want to be making decisions yet you're still sitting into a stock and waiting for a crossover. Right here you can see the zoo is with a minus right here. It's with a minus. How is this? That's a solid signal because minus means crossover has happened now right here. I will tell you to sell now very short. One point. 1 6 4 6. So it's like minus 1 point 1 6 4 6 4 to perfectly pay Pip if you remember.

So profit will be 25 percent. Isn't it because we have created one great trade and now in the third grade all the waters are gone and we are in profit off 35 papers now. We lost the max on the straight and Pip's. Now if you have earned that five point profit then this means we have to do a bad trait in our pocket. So we don't have to worry about the team because those trades will be colored by our game plan. And if we understand to keep this profit 10 a little tyke will always be in profit because at the end of the day you're looking your account as a company and if your company gives out a dividend every quarter let's presume you are on the thirty five Pip and you give out a profit to yourself as a group. That means paying off your company's profit and your network.

Blake automatically in Kaysing health microcell whenever it counts. That's not a good move. But you'll always see this kind of confidence fall into that trap. This is the perfect trap as I created this trap when a rake is falling. I can hit a small bite and mostly I can't Agosto sure you are HUGE buying but they are not getting fixed. Because basically what it does is places like 2 million buying either a million dollars by an order and in front of it you play a $100 buying order so that one stock gets you see a million buying order and then certainly 100 or like jumps in front of it or 500 odd jumps in Frankfurt. So basically it's showing you but you're not getting paid because basically sometimes 100 are jumping in some time to top that are jumping in like basically someone is camping in front of it and slowly and gradually after a few seconds that you know are like autos gone.

So you presume it's got fit but it's not. It was just shown to me dear. And the price ran up on the assumption that somebody is starting to jump in. But no big blows here. Remember Beckler is here. And if you look at it now and we see the captain dropping and now it's only going up. So now it's like a position at the beginning. Why? Because the price has gone above. Pulling up. And even though he hasn't crossed out, I would buy at one point one 664 like matka at one point 1 6 6 4 and the next year it crosses up. And if you look at it it did cross up to buy all the weight it did fall off. But don't wait because it's in a good mood. However it drops off right here when it opens it or where it drops off. If you look at the building of a mine you know pointed out that was it.

So minus means. So so so on this day or in the mind this won't sell. So at one point 168 one point twenty five make one point 1 6 5 8 6 PAIP loss. So from a profit you have gone back to profit or and profit. But if it opens you it comes back to fill up and you can like sit on it to get what I call a breakeven great project. When 0.26 felt it all happened at one point when I made bucket art I got up one six 6 full so you can get it. But let's follow the plan. Don't let's not go to the favorable things like school the bad things because pivotal things are good for you. So it doesn't matter what makin's just bad things because they increase you're upset once you're out on this hour then you fight and fight.

Now please please please remember that destroyed within the day. So it isn't like telling you to come off as a day trader. It's not a problem. But now if you look at it far off I know crossing out that by artist signal but that's a clear signal. And I usually tell my students to pay more for this kind of bile loop. And what he's saying too by the price is near doubling of buying. Everything looks good but makes me sick. This is the worst day ever. Why? Because of your selfies I'm lost. Why? Because first of all there's no telling no off a CD so it's not a great trade. Second if you just focus on the cake. So we make money right. Right you cranked up. So we were thinking of making the money and it was going well.

It opened lower and like our trade I get like I get on the toilet and it hasn't closed above to put it back in a window because so much in your neck it could have but you did it like. Opened it closed, no doubling back. That's the first sign that there's something wrong. Two I won't bite. Right. But if you look at it it did fall off and now it's like going up. Now in net it's always a room but you should have a plan B if you're not following blindly then what is your plan B your plan B is once the price crosses doubling up and on top of you buying it if it crosses up on the Kills on the hourly kind of kills. Now if you look at it the price continues to go up but it's not closing above doubling of number one. Number two you're buying order was far higher if you wrote a book on the fall on the red line then I would have told you to buy it on the why.

Because first of all if the price won't cross double up on top then Best Buy is the 16 highest buy and it's a lot to trade because the price won't care if you fall. And in the fall I would be having a huge loss as my buying prices are so high if it were worth cross-compiling abandoning for the goodbye. But if it hasn't, Danuta is locked to take because it's at the highest point in time by the highway and you know it won't be clogging up dacoits. If you were to have Parcak here on a direct line then I would call it this as a breakeven rate. And I would have jumped on this slope in the open. Sorry not on the open because the open is higher but on the close region it's on the red line. So it's not that bad.

That's a kind of a position that may break even if the plan fails and the building goes down. And if you look for the pooling goodbye and continues to grow up and the price continues to go up slowly and gradually but it's not gotten on the upside. And therefore your order is still the same example or I take one point 1 6 7 0 and Carrick's one point 1 6 7 3. So it's only a profit but the risk is increasing. And the CD continues to like to reduce the gap. And any it can just go down and get a cell signal and right here. And we are at a loss. If you were to have market care at one point twenty six hours you know and here is one point 1 6 6 5 6 or 5 plus again but we never bought it because we knew it should have closed higher and it didn't.

So it was not good but a playground for late on this day you would have not DAY Target because there was not a good sign to go on to the trade so for my learning point of views are you have to remember you are here to make money and you can see even though on doubling of it and once it was within the building of mine you never made money on these two tracks. And if you remember this trade we never made money on this either. So a contractor building up is not good only if you can buy on the red line or on the labeling and then I would call it a good buy order. But if the price goes below doubling up then it's also a sign of concern. But the point is to remember what is happening and trade accordingly. Now in the next chapter we will discuss and choke on the Euro U.S. dollar and I will explain to you how to trade that. Thank you.

EURUSD 30M Day Trading

Hi guys today you will this your you're stronger. But on the totem in your. Now you can see these at the buy orders that you placed on the hourly chalk. Now I will switch on to the 30 minute chart for me. Go now. Test focus again. It has automatically brought us to this chart. And what do you see then error. There's a higher chance to make money and a higher turnout. Because first of all the price was the most important point and there was a huge gap that could have made that money and went to cost up that it was a higher chance for the next moment. Now it has dropped again. But if you focus on density It's like a line if you could pick your slyness in two words to seem loath which is a good sign and it's slowing down rather than a steep fall like this it's not having a steep fall. Right. Which shows you that it's a good moment in time as it tells you that a good pie order can be placed.

So if you're thinking of short selling and we're seeing this kind of position then remember that's not a good moment for a short seller because it is starting to seem pretty close. Bad moment now for a shark show selling below the building of a band that turned out to be cute right. But I always tell my students that buying is far better than chalk, sorry. I'm not shocked that short selling is bad. I don't believe it's a bad thing. I believe it's a good thing because in the fall the only buyers in the market are the short sellers. They buy in the fall. No other person is willing to buy. They are the person who brings buying and bringing stability. So I don't think of them as a bad person but I believe the short selling offer is a higher risk than buying it. It's easier for the price to go from $1 to $2 but from a dollar for a short summer the highest point of profit is if the price falls from $1 to 20 cents.

Now I don't believe like below 20 cents because I believe that once the price goes below 20 cents then the percentage fall increases because from St to reset it's only 2 cents. But the percentages tax again putting forth. And therefore I believe that's the tricky stuff and you don't usually make money below 20 cents. So my concept is from a dollar. It's only an 80 percent profit but the risk is far higher. Because if the price moves above the dollar then you have a higher risk because the price can go unlimited risk. But on the buy the risk is far lesser than the short sellers. So now let's look at what's happening now to continue the crossover. And that machine is going down down down down and now it's crossing up right here. One point one 5 5:8 bucket at one point one in five to. No place to Eicken right.

And one point twenty seven one point 1 7 5 0 0 0 by moment. Now our first major target is this high bringing about so don't expect huge sums of money now at least from one point twenty five to. It's only going to the same profit and I don't pay 20 percent because it's reducing its firing so quickly for the profit is approximately 10. Max because if you look at it now it's one point twenty five one point twenty seven town five apps the next day. Again good news again and again even though the price is getting higher and higher. Mike Stalock is easy. And the concept is to say that's the highest point and now it's like going flat. So your profitability chart at the moment is limited but when you follow the embassy the reason is that now it's jumped up.

Boom boom boom. It goes up. Up and up. And when it has a higher IQ. And now jumping on what. So the best thing ever. And that's why I trust him because it offers the pastry cook. Now this is just one trade. Now my. And the daytrader you have to exit at a moment in time and that exit would have been like we find out right now in that case I enter data and what do I sell here. And the next open I jump up to buy now a pair has so much volume that you can buy and you mount it in a second. So that's not a problem. The only thing to remember is to be on your seat half an hour before the open. Now training doesn't stop. So the concept is on the prettiest clothes you suddenly have. And then you suddenly flip and by the next moment because your time changes and the day triggers 19 years.

So by continuous you jump up so basically for the day that you sell and the next moment you buy so that you don't have to face those overnight fees. It jumps up, up , up and up. Now currently there are many brokers that offer those fees so you can look for them as well. So it goes up up up. It's still bullish. But now the files have started to increase because once it was posted I think it moved. It was for respect. So it is not broken. This kind of law was not broken. It was not broken. This was not broken but this rule is broken. The disputes the claim made stopped and that's where it can sell because if you look at it it's minus $0.02 the other zero minus minus. Sal and you would also like some product here one plate went down 5 0 and 30 Carrick one point twenty two to one. Now all right you make about one point eight to one.

So it brings up a 51st. So if on profit 51 per profit plus the profit we naturally like it and I really countered. So they make a profit. And by doing what. Nothing. Even you and profit. How did we get any good test within two days? Nothing special. This is the second day. It's going up, up , up and up and right. It's the last game of the day. So you go up and this was a time when you were already thinking of getting out. So it's not something special. It was already time for you to get out as a day trader and you went out and if you look at it for the price still falls off still falls off still falls off. But right here it goes straight. See Why. Because if it still falls further down that he can maybe cross below the building again. And that brings short sellers.

So the price of booze and not being an opportunity for others goes straight. If you look at it, it's still going straight down if it is for you right now. But no, I'm just cocky to contract and that's a good thing for buyers because I want to bring the bank to contract so that the new opportunity is good and great. You could buy a signal again. One point when Tony tells Let me interject one point so an 8. And like me being an icon and just looking at it right here your body. So let me bring the guy further cooking presence and cross the line on top. Now Dr. godmamma. All sounds are made in Australia as well and it can include those increases in cruel does include this. And then at the moment it goes below the red line.

Dr. Cross. And right but the movement to look at the price is forming a double top this up and just up. It's approximately the thing. And if you look at my TV The highs are getting your That's a bad thing. So always and to date you know these are your signs to tell you what the next day trading will be because every day trader is willing to learn information before time. Now onto your forming a complete set of plans that I have found by using thousands of dollars but I've gained tons of money to do it as well. And that's the reason you are following the plan. But you have to look for clues to understand what the future holds because basically it's our plan that works on the median bill of the bank.

But we have to have an understanding because as a good trader you don't jump into the plan every day. Some days you ignore it. It's simple. I just told you an example. At the end of the chapter off one hour the euro U.S. dollar chapter that we had never seen. Even low or MSEE you are seeing us to buy. But we know what it did. That's the thing I will tell my story. MSCE is great but you have to use the go ahead to get in or out. And even if you believe yourself that it's a risky trade no matter what there is is some extremely bad news. And will see the same buy that doesn't go into the truck because by this book I'm showing you examples like tons of examples you can see it works every time. So the concept comes in. Why risk it. Why not wait for a few days.

If you believe there is something wrong. Yes. You were there Ali. You might use Tony Pep's but the concept is to create one you believe in. That's the biggest concept example. We're talking to you at one point when Tony 8:7 answered it. At one point when it went to making a profit I mean this was one pip and this is going to be pep do it it's a 70 for profit one to create.

And this was a robot and that was ending just after a few hours so it was clever. And then you make yours. And the price went up and now this is all to the closing of the day. So you have made a good profit from getting up. I go out and buy it right away. You are concerned now. It goes up. Now you were buying it. May I ask. I was telling you to be concerned but I'm not telling you to buy on the cross or my own heart.

Why am I taking that risk when you are like I think your instructor is telling you to be vigilant and I'm still telling you to buy everything. Always remember to remember Vi you are considering going to the thing that many traders forget and lose money. I didn't start to be concerned because this is a double top and everything was coming right back on this high cost. So that thing is gone now. And on the ground any time was near the top. So I'm betting building a city across the bay crossed or off like it would be hired high. And the next opportunity. So the concern is now gone because these highs can cost this high and that is like paying more buying won't it. So my big concern is to go straight stroke stroke when he goes straight. That's not a good sign.

And it goes to take what you can do anything. You are simply out now. This is, I believe , a lost trade. You brought it here at one point 24:6 one point twenty eight six minus one point twenty eight for one. So it's a five day plot. Now if you remember we had a sound For-Profit and we have now a five year process. So we're still 69 per profit. That's how the game works. Your losses should be you make it back to make them limited. You have to split the second shop. So if this scandal and at Tony Bennett for the second your trade should be like mine. Was it? It is starting to enter the game. You are starting to trade. You should not be waiting for 10 years. It's something that you have to do automatically. You don't fit into the stock.

See the price. Now it's going straight, it's going higher. My take is going straight straight straight and boom it goes lower once it goes lower. What happens? Shocked sellers come take but I won't suggest you cracker jack even for short sellers. I always tell them to always look for higher ground. If you find sharks selling to be appropriate. Actually on the deal you know don't jump up in my chalk. You have to find a high loan to make the trade on a lower level. Now this is one point 8:32 Chucho pricey the price moves up. This is a bit shocking. That's exactly it. And now I am not pleased I can to shock sell but I am just shooting what can happen. Now this is also one of the best techniques to me just how much profit you flip it how you flip it.

You make sure they get crushed below. So they're short sellers. You go short sellers come then short. So you make the price or not panic because it's a huge loss. From one point twenty eight to nine one point one it five. That's a twenty one pay plus the panic and the buy and wants to buy blue flip it now a game piece is a buy signal. But when I buy, if I remember the last five minutes I told you not to buy and at this moment you shouldn't talk on the phone about when you met or that you could have jumped up too close. It didn't if it didn't. That's the highest risk coding ever. But by making the price falls on the red line. Let me jump in. OK. It isn't because the red line offers breaking even trade contests. It affects human trade.

So I'm a buyer. I can at one point twenty four six PIANTO one point twenty eight for six and the price moves see you about ten. And then next year or so it's say 90 plus. OK. You make that last because you have so much money on the table that you have no way because you made it for the last five last night. So it's 14 years plus. Not a bad trade. It's still a 60 per cent net profit. So remember this year we'll be getting this kind of creation. Now right here it's saying buy and that's best buy ever because it's crossing a building well. So you buy it at one point twenty six. And it moves higher and higher. But just look at this highest point that was never reached here.

It's like a sport where I can look up and move up what Method is pointing to the highest point right here. This is the highest point and it's just Chivery and going down. That's not a good move. Now don't just move around to sell but I won't tell you to sell it to external property. You can put a stop loss on display. That is the extreme. After the slow back because you have budgeted so you can play sick. It goes straight and it points lower. Now your group does slow to a stop loss. You simply sell it, cancel it and sell it. As simple as that one point twenty seven eight right.

And you bought it at one point 186 no. So you have placed a strong one point 1 8 6 0. Minus one point one point twenty eight thousand eight. So again making a profit. Now if you remember most about crakes Kraker floating Peppe and making a profit so it's a net profit 78 Pipp profit. This is how the trading goes because you clearly showed me so much profit that you are back credit should be absorbing and how Pip's item by making sure you are trading a good trade.

EURUSD 5M Day Trading

Hi guys today you will discuss your story appearing on a five minute chart. Now before I begin the chapter I need to give you a warning now. Five minute sharks is something like playing with fire. Now as you have seen previously in all my chapters you concede that this strategy works easily and its results are extremely limited. Now the same thing will happen in the fight against the shock doctrine. The problem is it moves all over the place so it can be that you can have five or seven losses and then a good profitable trade to wipe the slate clean to get no losses on the net basis. So it's a net profit to Bear Creek Park.

There are many claims that we have to bear with them. The second thing you have to be quick no matter what trade is going to create going against you. You have to be quick to take whatever Craig knocks on the door. Now what I mean by Dr I mean no one I picked no one should come in and dystopian you should have really you should have bought it you should have everything in it and it's like a locked door. No one came in because it took five me crazy in five minutes. You lost your focus for a second and you lost. Craig, that's as simple as that. Because it's so fast it's so fast that it was like a split second difference.

Example. Let me show you right here. You can see me make it big. You can teach jumping in but make it small. The highest Mormon kid dime is. Mr. King can't be a discontented district coward. You can now usually add that split second Sometimes it is for sure that it does cross-culture and the price will be showing it both cost up to one to choose at basically as per plan. You'll be taken to buy Bach. It's not a complete candidate. It made the candidate find the candidate to be completed before completion. So you have to wait for the last second. You don't have to open the window and break within the last 15-20 seconds so that you have to order ready one to five and it goes, let's take 10:30 at 10:30. You work for a second. Your honor should be placed.

It should be as quick as that reason because this is exactly what happens. It will give a close call but the next day it opens and boom it goes down. So you have to wait for the closing of the candle so that you can see it now close higher and then it falls off. That's the number one thing. Number two is sometimes losses. And then you have to again be a skulking person who doesn't care about losses or profit. He only cares if he follows the plan or not. You have to be vigilant and have to be ready. You have to be sure you see a plan that says tell you're simply so you don't make you don't care you make money or lose money because this thing that you made money or lost money is at the end of the day at the end of the week at the end of the month at the end of the quarter loss our profit. It's not today.

Never never never. If the talk comes into your mind again and again then don't take five minutes. And then as I told you I lost focus means a loss in trade that's as simple as that because this is a five minute chalk. It works so fast. You may not be able to make money. So if you cannot keep it closed then don't take five men Jack. If you cannot keep the last talk I will see that you get lattes or you'll have lots of up like a trading day. And don't take it as simple. To talk should not be there. No one should come in to do it no matter what next. Now the next stock trading plan. If I just mean and move here, that's the best opening. The first number right here is that it's a quarter or right one point. You will be buying it.

Let me play it right here. Let me do my bit. So here bucket here. Now you can see the e-zine now that you sign your shows are you worth Baker. Hugs are easy to make out. Now discounts usually are helpful. But don't take a break from what you make. I ask Howard to help. Now I won't comment on the speaker's hugs while they count but if I come in here Frakes daughter hired at the worst shut down. And now you know if you don't and then it is good news for the dollar because the bad news for the dollar with us shut down. So it's like a simple play news that told you it was right back for the oil company. It depends on the full cost and when you do respect. So it's not as good news as the shutdown news is, just like you have to understand a different psychological effect of the news.

They are helpful but we'll be following your plan. Number one no it states that the news came here but your turnaround is already here. See you are already buying it. So this tells you that you are on the right track because you have to at that point. So are the common retail investors who will ask the question again and again why the price rose and to make best who will pay them this news. They began to freak out when the price rose up but that is the case. I couldn't believe it because you would see it again and again and I've seen good news coming. But the price will be falling off. So how come it's like rising and falling off the second time. That's the plan, come in because you have to be ready for the circumstances. Now you're buying at one point two to one. Let's move to Florida.

Now as you can see up to the news price goes straight down when it comes in. First dollar set for biggest weekly gain in more than a year as Stirling's slump. Now if you look at it based on the U.K. piggish pound sterling but basically it helped us understand what is happening in the global space. Now you're creating your U.S. Europe here. So it's not fair that Apoc if Craig can pound is having just been making out to be facing that same thing now as you can see the thing is crossing up but your price is not courting. Now if you are a member of the chapter I told you I could be the ruler of this kind of crazy and you should be. But that is a slight difference. Stop pulling the baddies further apart. So you couldn't expect a smaller profit. And that's exactly what is happening.

But Edward drove up rather than stopping at the building and it crossed up on the five next chalk. So it tells us that a further eye is coming in and that's exactly what happened. See it rises up false christ up back again fault rises up back again. But now it's again going straight now straight trading ranked. It won't be making news like big money but you have brought it here at one point to one fall and it's currently trading at one point KOO-KOO to nine. So it's a 15 percent profit and awesome profit. And external Polish. So you remain bullish but you need to be like what you like as the price gap between the red and blue line is extremely limited. So you have to understand that anyway it continues to sell the next thing you know best. Pulling up and is completely contracted. So it means that you may not be making up like the poor from now on.

So you just need to be vigilant nowadays and then he may chase after her using a speculative neck and a promise for one forty eight point seven. Now X fourteen point eight thousand not do this kind of news does affect what it tells you speculative fiction. But if you look at it to price a stock between the banks whenever you get stuck It doesn't tell you a good picture. Now if you look at it often it wasn't a cell signal it's generic right here. It's minus zero point zero zero zero so minus means sell. And we simply sell by member. You have to be there Sellick within the first and second because as your time goes you'll lose money. So if you have sold it at one point go to teach me. So we simply minus at one point two to three. And he made a nice profit from buying and selling. That's pretty good right now.

Our next check comes in. And if you look at it it made minus water and plus water and the cost was above the bootlicking Gobind as well. So it's again a Polish cost. Simply buy it here. Now if you look at it the next five years could open nor could have made a profit would have been like saved and it fell off. Gosh the red line this red line PLF best threadlet and now striking back up again. Riding driving and rising sea and you're making easy money. And it fell off. It's only 0 and this is minus. So on discounted yesterday you're buying it again next off. Now five minutes is great for the trading season. You're going to be allowed to disclose because it's so cool. It's such a short time that you don't need to worry about that.

Just look at it. This is five 10 15 20 25 30 35 40 45 50 55 60 one hour five 10 15 20 25 one hour and 30 minutes and your trade is out. So shocking. So this is why people love a five minute jog on the day trading basis. But I always tell my students please

please please remember that you cannot trade and forget five minute creating means you can do that black. Now in this trade you made a pay profit and now if you look at it we are going to keep it profitable. Krista Tippett It's like profit in our bank and it's a profit that will help us fill the last several gaps because basically loss is part of the game. You just need to make sure that your property is so high that you cannot buy in your like logic. It could be that the market should give you a 50 year profit and then take back 20 per profit.

So you are still net 30 per profit. It should not prove that you are minus 10 Pipp by a member. You need to keep on trading. It is not a game for it to be cocky and five ex-Special is not a game for the COGIC now itself to sell what happens next. It sells tell tell tell tale and it plays by right here. Yup this is a plus point. No, its minus still minus. Next day is still minus because if you look at it I'm putting my mouth on showing you're minus a plus. And so it's still minus minus minus. So you cannot buy it again. And that's exactly what you need to see. What's mine is mine is mine is mine is mine. Once I go here it changes. So you have to keep at it the most whether it is to see the correct picture and fault falls fault price rises higher and it's falling.

Now if you look at it it's not enough so second man see now d'Espagne never helped you now how you and now saying crossover. Now if you look at it this Crossthwaite does happen on this news. Irish consumer confidence which is actually better than the previous. So it's a good thing. But the point is you have to follow the plan because there is good news. I boost for an extremely short period of time. So if I come in I take what I do to help. So the news is good but it's not selling or supplies going. No one can stop it. Because if someone is better then you have to bring in so much buying and selling. So good news can be turning to bad news and especially under-five you Chuck. I can tell and within the next 15 minutes I can buy my stock. I can buy my Schrock. So now at one point I try one point two to five three and we go higher. False. False right.

Higher false rises high rises higher and right itself on the last green candidate. So you sell it to a profitable trade. It's still a profitable trade. You bought it here at one point two to five three. So Rick at one point did so in five. So it's like minus 1 point to do so in five. You made 22 payments a day. So you're making profit on all 28 and it's an exceptionally profitable trade. Remember the game is simple. You have to follow the plan but the game changes once the price goes a doubling the in on the lower side and to fall off signal. So as of now it's not crossing on the lower side it's still like it's always crossing and upside right here right here and right here. And when Eric crossed on the upside you made a good profitable trade.

But it remains the same: you cannot let anyone in the know be close. If at this moment someone came in and you couldn't sell it. Then you can panic the next time. And you can use money at any time right now. You might say I won't sell it, it will go up. Yes you're right. But the point is why take the risk. The rule of thumb remains. Why take the risk. Because once you lose the plan you are all on your own and no one can stop you because basically the blind works on end to end it now ruction between. So you have to work on the moment that means you sell. Otherwise you will get stuck. And if you look at it the price still goes straight and Grosch on the upside.

Now although I'm not saying a bad thing but I mean I buy now what's my stop loss. That's this red line blue red line is my stop loss.

And if I want to put an extra action stop loss then if time me like slow right. That's my actual stop loss action stop just means that if it breaks the law then whatever the price is I would get up because basically it's not a car yet so I have to have a plan that can sell or buy not for anything dire fall far off you're still here. And this is minus all right here. And it sells right. One point to our buying rate was right here. One point to do a three minus one point to do a two to one pay plus. But the point it's almost you could use your losses to a few Pipp. That's the number one rule if you want. You will have a hard time jumping back again today and crossing up to signify Melmac right here. At one point two to fall and price fall off for a start goes lower.

Well now one check for gas this is the. Now this is what I call the last habitat but you have to accept this is part of the plan. Don't ever like to say no. I want to tell you it will come back because if you will, that's the stock for like mist or for a mistake that won't be corrected for a long time. Now if you bought it at one point to fall and all that at one point to do 8:4 wait one point to Knightfall minus one point to a four. Yeah that's a paper loss that's huge. So this is how you learn Knightfall, a full time plot that's a huge cost. But that's part of the key. You have to bear with it. And if you look at it you saw a lot and the price even touched one point two.

So that's extremely low. This is why be vigilant and open your eyes because if you weren't sweating right here you might have a lawyer like by price. And if it breaks this can go bad then you can have even lower your losses. Well people like to pile up and be extremely high. So always make sure that your losses are extremely limited. Now this is a 10 page plot but if you look at our profit it was all within 20 percent 15 18 percent that was double of what our maximum loss our biggest loss is. Thank you.

USDCHF 1h Day Trading

Hi guys, take on this US dollar Swiss franc on a 16 minute chart. That is a one hour chart. Now why am I doing this Swiss. Three guineas. Most of the example big companies usually hide their money in Switzerland and to hide their money they need to convert them from us or any other country into Swiss franc and try the buying constant buying in it because to save taxes you hide them in an offshore company and basically docked money become tax free because wherever you invest from so frank that is the profit will it done. Interesting Frank because it's interesting how to explain that if I am like sending $50000 to the land based account and then I'm investing that $50000 into let's say in Great Britain and in Great Britain I will be showing it off as an Englishman coming from Switzerland.

So therefore when giving a loan to another of my company in Great Britain then that will return back to swizzling. And therefore my buying into the Swiss franc will remain constant. I think U.S. talks with Frank are in Great Britain Frank but basically so that will act as my gateway. However now many many countries have come to take or steal the pollution from society but it still remains an important market and therefore you must rollerskate Frank you maintain important Forex pairs. Now look any further. As of now just look at it. If I make it pick the most are getting broken and the highs are not getting crossed. Now this is an important tool. Please please please remember this whenever you see something like this be extremely bullish.

Even if you buy dên all to be vigilant put stop losses please stop losses. Don't treat it just like that. Remember it's in a downtrend now under Ray Kelly. Some might say high above decide yes it is but it meant I both fell off and made a second bad move. And you think about it. Now I should not have come back now. It should have cost cost cost and then like below this high it might have moved down. But it should not have come up like this high. If a date ever did right this fall it was a bad move. The second prize was a fake crisis and never crossed the first rise. So remember this stinks. Now let's move further to our trading plan. Caressa right. You're planning for a run. So you will bite me so I can write to you.

Now some of you may too. Why I started off right here. You can read the full article right here. That's your point. I like then the cell signal would have negated my plastic front and by signal laws 9:5 for not to store the stuff for profit even if I look at the price. It looks as if it's going straight. It's not going up it's not going down not making a huge lake difference but to make a profit. So the concept is that the plan works. Righto I pointed out that the price doesn't look to be making money. It looks to be X-Gene, your fake one that's how you will make money. That's the power of this plan now. Yeah I bought it at night for show and run lights. Me kicked point 9 4 7 1 and 2 feet it folds ghost like no great falls straight.

Now if you look at it the craving is going straight now as it was discussed. Whenever there was anything by and the prices going straight that's not a good move. But remember the gaps. Now as if now you have a small gap on the top side. Killed a couple in the back but on the boat side. Kinda broken bullet in the bandboxes smaller gap and the point of a higher chance of growing up. Now it didn't it went down down down but to be across or no it never now. Anyway my mouse moves into this space. I see a wrong signal right here but follow that follow up and it goes till the end line. Now I still pass on this moment. It was told no it was not mindless drivel. It was zero.

And the next day. Oppenheimer. Now whoever was creating the spare room at this moment could drop down and it would go down. So make sure that you can open time by buying more fabric. Yes you are a Swiss franc at the moment because that's why I want to put it all in an hour or two for the same purpose. Maybe not following the same plan that I am discussing here but their plan is something I don't want to display. It may have different rules but they're following the same stuff and you can see it right. This is a huge cap and it makes a cap at an extremely crucial time. Why would you do that? And if you look at it, it may get high and now it's crossed off to go back down. Does that now mean you have a higher chance of making a good profit?

But now it's going straight. It crossed her and told her it was great training by quite getting the hang of it, making junk up so that to vote for the crossover and follow the straight trading plan. Now although the state couldn't plan it is like a four telling sign that there's something wrong but you will vote for confirmation you'll never jump in before confirmation. Now whenever I tell you that this is the problematic sign what I'm going to say is you need to be very you make to be ready. If my cell takes me to come then I will tell because basically for us which means many of mine could be. And that's right. These are the things that make us like being close, although we're not falling back. It's like the yellow traffic sign off to a red light.

No, I didn't mean to go. Like I said I don't go. But you can go. But there's a killer to be ready. That's the yellow sign of straight trading. Like it has more. Higher and higher. Now if I crossed this high it crossed this I. Know if I could make it big. It fell off. But Fell off like coming into the domain of these guys. No, it never costs higher again. And now it is costing this high. So next move further. It stops right back up again back up again. Stops go straight. And now it's about across town and here you get it. Mine has a gym as you. So it's so right here at Cedar Point and excelling like me at the sale right here. You know point nine five six so when I come here it's minus little point 9 5 6 7 8 9 6 profit ninety six put profit on a day profit. That's huge. Extremely well. And that's the reason I will tell my students to focus on the group of experts.

Now the Swiss franc is a good fire expert. Haven't I just told you it's basically a good flight for people to hide money now people from all over the world from China, Hong Kong or other places to hide money. And mostly the poverty as you mentioned are and is including Switzerland too. Frank is one of the countries where they hide the money. And for them it's like you have to buy Swiss francs to hide in Italy so you'll make sure that you try this and it automatically rises because there is a continuous buying coming in. Continuous demand is here. And that's the reason it makes such a good profit not to sell right here. So sell. But if we're looking at the price jumped up straight up I'd like it to buy. Why because it's grouching the building of an older MSEE was a breathtaking crossover from my point all right to the mistakes.

Plus the real point that I want but the point is if it costs up that's a good moment to buy a plan 9 5 9 1. You bought it late and it jumps back up Frausto that A-line likes to slow. And now it's right back up again. And it is across. We're right here on this camera. So you sell now. Diane focus's it for 40-45 minutes. Talk about five 10 15 20 25 30 35 40 45 minute and bought the body care act point. 9 5 9 6 9 5 9 6 minus. We sold it here at little point 9 9 6. So it's a high point of $960 six. So it's perfectly brilliant isn't it. 9 5 9 6 and yep and a profit. That's how it is. But now what's the results that we are seeing first my second now and not jumping down the stairs as that a good honeymoon period is about to end.

And be vigilant because it's slow and it's still falling off. It's not a by fact on the price Tony we're seeing it was going straight. Now if it would have cost on the lower side below the building of I don't it would have been like a major cause of concern that maybe kind of stuff like right here it costs on top crossing in the bank on this day. So it was a bicycle ride at 0.9 6 for right here. You have Ruddick and it jumps up jumps up jumps up but it jumps down and it's a cell signal right. Now the thing to note please remember once the price of Karasu is troubling then they will spread issues by spreading. I mean that the buy and sell price will be great and that it might be bigger. So sometimes you might not be able to jump in at this moment.

Now what is the solution to it? The solution is if you can't then ignore that great. Now what am I trying to tell you? I'm trying to tell you that let's do it in a month. You can make 50 Craig but Greg issues. You cannot make those 50 then make 30 great ones but make them at your disposal rather than running after the price because right here you have no point nine six one four. And they take it point 967 to scrape a profit. Now what that. I prayed last that you can except I would say 4:57 they don't go beyond that. It isn't. You have to accept them as you are late now right here in between these buy and sell the minute I put Adderall wrong I couldn't now right in between buy and sell you've made a strong profit of 20 to pay up. Now if you own this place you're seeing a two to five up Gap spread then I would suggest you can dampen to take the pipe is not a huge loss basically are losses that are on the scene like band toxify pep.

But if it goes beyond that tactic then it can boot camp and like Lucky lead to. Without you it isn't because you have seen as my training plan that Max profit in a five minute chart is around 30 40 50 50 Peppe it has given us a 100 per price. But you have to understand though like when I call the problems the profits are 15 -20 Tampere , the smallest profit. So you cannot tape on the spread your spread should be at and by spread I mean by self-pride spread. So on this moment when it's soon you can buy them at the last second you will open your buying lingo north expect to jump on to the files thinking great but not beyond that like to create movies about you but don't put extreme strain on it. I take five PAIP is what I call the max spread I can accept. But the ideal thing is to buy on the price. So remember that this is your game plan.

Now if you look at it it's a cell signal and the price continues to go straight now going straight on a signal is always a sign. The reason we're going to sell means that the price is falling off but it's going straight. So it means someone is buying. And that's a good sign. All right. It is a buy signal. At 1 9 6 7 1. So let me market you to a six on one and let's go forward. Now here you go. It goes straight for a few days. Sort of sorry for a few five minute cantles and right here to selfing. So you just wait to see the cell signal. If you see a light sell signal right here you get out of computing. Now if you remember Muskie on the rise it was tops on direct . So you might at this moment be confused and you might think it's a stop or and the price will jump up but whenever it just sells I would suggest you can sell now this moment is 0.9 thinks it's one.

So it's the low point ninety six x1. That's a 10 plus. So except that and the SEC on the sidelines. The reason it falls and breaks the second low tech X at the top. Now this didn't hurt at all. So it makes up what I call the total formation. Then when you see four pops and all falling down then that's a bad signal. And the price falls below the Willinger bank for the first time. You haven't seen that in our trading for the previous two days and this is the first time back signal the price comes back up. Go straight and right here it is the red line. But if you look at the first two Croswell numbers it's still minus right here. You look at it if it is minus. That's not your normal day you'll wake outside it falls off fall off fall off fall off and on this time it's still minus. But here it's plus 0.01 that means you can buy.

But as I told you earlier it's a falling market right here. It was four tops, two doctors, two tops and falling. So it's not a good market to trade on. So all this trade which Stop-Loss losses either on the slow or on any of the major low risk discounting like and you know stop losses. Twenty one put in action star crossed at a price. So if you break it slow right here you will out price jumps higher. Go straight go straight go straight. Now I look at it at this moment you're expecting the price to go higher than just pulling a bank but it never did. That was a bad thing. And at the end of the day their message across town and seeing a cell signal boom right at Graaff down. This was a positive negative that is negative 0.01 pamphlets to sell signals. And it's a lost trade. Stocks are dictating gawks, remember this and make the money. Thank you.

USDCHF 30M Day Trading

Hi guys too they will discuss U.S. dollar Swiss franc when Todi minute chart and you will see how the trading goes. Now if you remember I've told you previously that whenever you see a double top on MECC that means a huge fall and it has fallen. Now whenever it falls, always look out for any other signal that tells you how much the fault lies. I look at it this is the extreme fall extreme and right now the embassy is the extreme lows which makes it a good buying see it even being because whenever it goes to extreme and it usually reverses now and we see something that doesn't go to like extreme and if it does and it like bounce back it's not something that goes to extreme mate.

And if you look at it it's IN the extreme means which means that you can expect the buying to come in now for buying too coming you need a crossover and Datsik this is to cross or now you'll be buying your on this day. Now all these like remember half the—in the market if you're trading a day trading and you'll be buying it. Now this is a 30 minute chart. So if you look at it, it's within the day. Now at this moment you will be buying it at 9 7 6 3. Here we go. Now let's look at it because it opens higher now. This always happens. I repeat this always happens that it opens higher and it goes for the high. Now you might say what do I mean by all this happening?

Now what do I mean by that is the lowest low whenever it is lowest low. Example if you look at it this is the lowest low. Now right here on the low low it tried to jump up to the highest point off putting up and see it dead. It fell off. It did. And right here it couldn't cross doubling off and so it fell off number one. So this opening was expected because we were expecting that it would touch the highest point in the building. Bad example right. So it's like understanding the game the game sees when it catches extreme lows it comes back to extreme highs. It fell off and then it was back. Now this selloff can also exist here. So if that is the highest point then it can go to the lowest point. But your aim should always be to look for what's happening. Now as you know we are creating Dickstein loads.

So you should have stopped losses on your first trading day. You will be on the lowest floor of discounting. Next it opened higher and fraud's for the next one and a half fiver. So this is the lowest point next to us. Toplessness comes here and you increase the stock prices accordingly. But just look at the profit loss ratio as well as the profits in cadenzas. Daniel stop losses become something of a novelty but do focus on what's happening now. Just look at it now. The thing to note is its growth backup and that's the high spike but now crossed it just as we thought previously in the previous month. And then it fell off. Now the time to know because the price fell off to the lowest level but ended up getting a bad contract.

Then your ability to go down becomes limited. So the stock cannot go down because as it is contracting you are seeing the downward limit. And even if it falls then it can fall to the lowest bank and as it falls. And this is a minus. If you look at the first number this is the minus 0.00 so we sold it here at the low point to fall and prettied up little point ninety eight to four. We made a 61 profit on the demon of chalk that's exceptional. However as a day trader day is a problem if the day ends right now as the day ends. So at this moment in time we just need to square off and the next Plake opening. You just buy it and the price goes up. However on the forex shock there are many brokers who don't fall for those who don't have the day trading problem.

They allow you to trade and they allow you to keep your position or not as well. Without any charge. So you have to look on to the brokers. But the point is even if you have a car then you can open it after that. And it's also a problem and you're earning a 61% profit. DECT huge debts exceptionally daks Surely if you are on the right track now for rises back up but the MSCE haven't done across all yet. So you wait and right here it's a crossover. If you look at it it's a plus. They opened a little and it crossed the Banas building of Banas. So it gives a good buy signal. But first let me place a sale like on now let me put in. I couldn't afford to buy a signal here at 1 9 8 5 0 and it goes straight and then jumps higher fault once it falls you'll be waiting for the minus sign.

Right here it's a minus sign. So the next opening right trait is your cell signal. So right here you will sell. Let me put Dyken here right here. And we bought or owned. I haven't marked Lekman market again. Wait a minute. Right here it is 0.9 at 5 0 minus We sold it to act 0.9 86 0. It's a 10 day profit huge without any problem. But the basic concept is you have to understand the basic concept to the basic concept is the best streets are these big want not the smart ones. But is it a stop or like a profit to stop. No they aren't. That is still too long. You would just wait for it to cross or and once it does it all right it looks to be crossing Yeah right Hayek's crossing.

So at zero point eight nine for nine you'll be buying it again. Now if you just focus on it all your rates are profitable. So the basic assumption of losses is out of the window. Now your aim is to just read again and again for this kind of a 61 year profit is huge on the 30 minute chart because basically what are you investing you're investing from photo-ID in the afternoon till the next day 4:00 in the morning. It's not even 24 hours. It worked. It's approximately 14 hours and you made $61 a profit. Automatically right here if you look at it it's the same. Only a few hours. And you made the money and the best part is there is still a gap left where you don't even trade. You don't even need to do anything. You just need to check the prices off a certain amount of sky.

That's it. And even if you don't have to wait, you will see the money train. Example if I just zoom out to just show you this is December and this is 50 tambour. Only two days within these two days. You have made a 71 percent profit. And if you walk further you will find that after just buying it is still pointing up. But it went up and now is pointing to a $.10 sell signal here. Now this is the first loss to buy. Craig now although I hate also will trade. But these are part of the plan. Now if you bought it where you one point ninety 8 4 nine. So let's make it zero point ninety eight for nine. Minus the selling price is zero point ninety nine point ninety eight twenty two it's a 10 plus. So for the 10 year profit. And this is a 10 year plus. So it's flat, nice to trade but the trade 61 per profit is still in our pocket. So on the net basis we are in profit. Now if we just zoom in.

What do we find? We find AWB needs on day Method not sure because it can fall from here and break. Like it's something to be vigilant off. Once you see a Double-O room it is a good buy signal example right here on disk crossover of building a brand. This meant that a Polish dime is here and he would have a quarter to nine point nine eight seven to boom and it goes flat for many hours. But then it jumps up and this is a cell signal right you know. Right. The whole point five so you select right here. Now all of this trade as well is not making a huge profit. This looks to be flat, opening a huge 7 0. It's a disappointing 5. There's a five year profit. But the point is you're all getting something out of that crate which means that your trade is not that bad you just need to play safe.

And this plan that I'm showing you that pooling abandoned theory is taxi plan which shows you that on the flipside on a bad day you are making five or 10 per profit or you're losing five or 10 per plussed to be profitable and last one Craig our breakeven themself and you are waiting for that one grade of six you and perhaps that will change the game so your aim is not always great. Your aim is not with huge sums of money. Your aim is just to get paid to playing again and again and again and again until you find one good crate and that one we're paid and you your tax because at the end of the day you are putting your hard on IN THE MONEY and you weren't really liking it that if you are not making money and for a day trader you need to understand that the basic problem with today is losses. And that's why I'm showing you this plan with money.

People like different things. Forex is totally different from stocks. In stocks do that your thoughts and dividend and stuff like that. In fact it's not. But still you can see that the plan works. But the point is to follow it again and again and again and again and not to second it. And if you look at it, just focus on it. You're right. I didn't get tix you fell off. And the last point is to say that 0.9 8 4 to 20 plus that you never make you out again. Let's see right here. If you're opening it tonight and the lowest point try it 0.9 8 5 6 to clean it up again. But you know never death doesn't come into your cup. What is a normal trader who doesn't have a plan.

He's trading all over the place and he doesn't know where to sell. But you as a new and intelligent creative investor Newsweek is selling get out and wait for the next good one to run and you are trading again and again with the same presumption. You buy, you sell and you aren't risking anything extra. Your Luck site your money invested. The main thing. You never increase it. I bet you never increase it. And your leverage. The most important fact of fall in Forex you managed to see if it was hundred percent right. It remains a hundred percent right. If it was 30 percent right here it means 30 percent Tricare what equity and peace that remain with the same game. And if you ask oneself then usually what do I do. I need my quarterly trade on the same amount.

Example I'm investing $100000 on myself and I'm taking a 30 percent leverage to $230000 and Torker even though my profits. In case you didn't pay a price here and I'm flat after that. So I paid at 12:54. My $180000 $30000 $250000 next to him. So I'm getting a $20000 profit so now my total money is hundred twenty thousand dollars. And if I gave a 20 percent leverage it goes to thirty six hundred fifty five hundred and fifty six thousand dollars. Right. But no you're wrong. I believe trade on a quarterly basis. That means that if you have invested yourself and 30000 in leverage then wait. If you own $20000 you can make it $120,000 yards and $10000 in leverage for that full quarter undercoating used to be like changing it if you have made $150,000 rather than $50,000 and take a person's leverage. But at the end of the quarter not before that it isn't because it creates distortion.

And I believe you should draw on your account as a company and as a company you should aim for the quarterly tax because tax all you will be able to do is your performance. I realize that's a distortion I like. Absolutely. Why? Because this step up after six to profit. They've been showing as profit in your tin cup and this 10 plus they were showing as a people loss in your account. Why? Because once you complete this trade we'll apply your total amount as $20000 for hire from $100000 it initially invested so your leverage in key 30 percent according to that. So your profit will be higher. The same way if you invested $20000 of your money and right here you are investing and return you to all of your money to a loss will exceed.

It won't be the same as the profiteer because your leverage is higher and your own money is higher. So to make it a simple method read late in the quarter great according to the quarterly game plan based buying is done 0.9 8:5. So Lexmark exceeded 0.9. He did 5 and moved forward now. What's best if it's acting at the exact point of building going bad. Now if you look at it this model number is the building burn top number. So this is zero point nine eight five. And the price ended at the same level. So it means it ended on doubling about now on doubling Gobind is usually considered Polish and that's exactly what happened as the price moved higher and higher. You're looking at a brilliant profitable trade. But now if you look at it this is an extremely touchy signal.

So you wait for the next 30 minutes and that's a crossover. So on the last five minutes of that 30 minutes you will be just squaring off because you already know they're just not pointing good. And I would like to correct my phrase if it's not the last five minutes of the last 30 seconds. So you have to open it by play order tap and within the last 30 seconds you just place it like a tray to complete the trade within that 30 seconds. You don't wait for it. But the best part is you bought it to actually 2.9 eighty five and you sold it as you deduct zero point nine to one. That's a 16 big profit, an exceptionally awesome reason because from 61 16 makes six seventy seven pips. And if I just zoom out, what do I show you? We started on toward December and distrait is 6 December. Within two days it's a Sony with a huge six per cent profit.

Within three days and you haven't done anything extra and slowly and gradually Vidlin like your trading plan your leverage will go to zero within that quarter. That's the best thing because you are paying with your own money. No one can dictate to you and therefore you're creating the best thing. And once that trading goes off on a quarterly basis then in the next quarter you again take that 30 percent leverage and you again trade it again and again and again until you complete it and that's how you run quarterly business. So that you yourself can generate and like and vote for you also and can tell yourself how much money you'll make. So that's how you will be running a complete company because trading in itself is a complex business so don't expect it to be not giving out dividends.

Tefal at the end of the year you have said. But the concept is to follow the plan. You can see that on our plan we made money then we liked it. It made 10 loft and 5 8:16 there. It was an 82 percent profit because of Fogarty's five steps. So an 8 bit profit is extremely good. You don't need to like to go anywhere to make that kind of money. It's exceptional. That's the power of taking it. But the contemporary main theme leverage is like a knife it picks in your hand you're powerful but if it's in your hand you want it able. Therefore I always tell you don't take the leverage to the next level. Try to keep it to a minimum , make it a quality trade so that at the end of the day you know what you made and what you lost because basic Popa is leverage should be used with extreme caution. Now in the next chapter of your list because a five minute jog of us star Frank to show you how our plan works in five minutes. Thank you.

USDCHF 5M Day Trading

Hi guys today we'll discuss a five minute jog on US Dollar, says Frank. Now the thing to note is I've made it extremely zoomed extremely back and I'm starting to show something extraordinary on the pipe and you can see the lows are getting higher this is higher this is higher. This is cool. This is higher. So the lows are starting to get higher which shows you that on the bull run this happens. But the price is getting low. Now it's a five minute chart so you will see this kind of divergence extremely like it will be extremely spread on. So you will have to understand what's happening because it's a five minute jog on a five minute chart. There will be many many many trading opportunities. There will be so many trading opportunities that you will be too old guard. And that's exactly what it is. Example right here except buy at 92 82 and it said sell here at 92 any fixed.

So it's for profit. But the problem is that only after 30 or 40 minutes it again said to you to buy at 92 61 and said to you to sell at 92 63 sorry 92 Yeah 92 63. Now the real problem is that Waseem now always remembers to stalk for a commodity or anything with extremely high volume. If you want to buy a thousand shares if you want to buy a lock off of 100 watt then you have to see that they should be a let's say on a five minute basis. They should be how the locks traded Dubai atol locked it should be $50 unlocked. Tony Dubai has the so they should be so much volume that you don't cut down on the spread.

55

Now what do I mean by don't cut out on the spread because as the volume gets decreased then there is a major gap between Dubai and the sell price and it's a bid and offer price and DAQ difference is what I see. That eats into our profit. So with any strategy either you follow my strategy or you make your own or someone else to do his own strategy I repeat any strategy requires extreme liquidity because as the spread gap widens then your losses are Chiquita's. Now I always suggest that don't ITP don't sell or two off money on the sprag if you see a closing price right Eric 1963 then I would suggest to do group to 90 to 60 or 292 or like three or five Pipp is extreme for desperate and you might take that but usually as the volume decreases.

So the spread increases. And if it's so much Breg that don't read the five minute chart because a five minute chart is something that is only reserved for something with tap extreme volumes. It should have so much volume that you are a thousand shares or your 2000 loss or whatever the trading you are doing should be extremely limited. It should not be shown live because if there is like a limited volume then the buy sell spreads the eat you up and add in the five minute creating the accreting extreme example from here deal there than here deal here. And if you look at it this is a walk of only six hours and two trades done. That's huge because that means within a day you'll be trading five or seven trapped and you'll be having this kind of choppiness as the seat said buyer I care 90 to 60 Nangle.

Yup it said by hared 90 66 and it said sell here 90 to 6 you've all exit to pay plus. So if you paid deep in the difference or to 5 for plus now five Peppe loss is not an extreme gosh I would live with it. But I always tell my students. Riley was important. You have to have some stock. Any fire expert. Extremely crowded otherwise ignore the deck for despair. Ignore decks' talk because for a day trader your liquidity is king. He can only make money if he lies. He was because you lose money you have with a brilliant plan. If there is more liquidity. And his plan seems to sell right at 90 to 63 and his Buy or big price is that let's say 90 to 60.

Then on the five minute Jack it's below the billing about now always initially told to get two to five Pipp is good but you have to look at it beyond that to five Pip and if it does I mean below the billing of an extremely irrelevant position because if you're buying if you're selling below the building of Anne and Lexi it says buy right here and you're buying a boat doubling up and then your profit is already gone. You cannot expect it to rise beyond pulling back every time. If you see all my previous trades there are many times that it stays within the building of the bank. So if you're buying a bubbling below Daniel that's a complete strategy and that's why I always look at the spread and then create if you're paying five minutes then be they're off to spread crap.

And I'm repeating it again and again and I will repeat it again and again because this is the biggest hurdle in making money. Now many of my students enjoy my strategy on an hourly chart 30 minute jog. Or any other chart but wants to move to 5 o'clock and there's no Walham and you are creating 10 percent of the volume in five minutes. Then that means they are doomed to fail. Although if they don't listen to me they make money sometimes. But the point is they make money sometimes not every time and other times they don't make money. They can be renewed and all their profits would be gone. In fact one great event right here you can see right here it says. Right.

But if my big price is not 892 six you can expect 90 to 58 then I'm selling below doubling back. And then it saves me to buy right here at Negat 261 but my Like offer price is at 90 to 71 and then I'm buying the above doubling back so my profits are limited to the billing a bad price. How can I make more money then I will be losing money on the ink on the like spread differently. And then after take off like commissions and all of the stuff said This brings to the question Are you ready for the five minutes trading. You've got five minutes trading is limited to an extremely good stock reason because it's really a problem with means once the price is within the blink of an eye and not once it's outside because once it's outside then you will be making a good profit.

And it might disparage a cost and that might give you a few pay profit but if you are making a profit and 10 Bips had gone to spread and commissions then half of your profit is gone and never trade in that market there you are paying half of the price and the cost of creating that means you're losing money. Now it's a Celtic Noreiga. I just look at it. They set sail right here at 92 68 and decided by Tricare 268 to flat. But if you're putting one on the spread price then it's a loss to Craig. And my assumption presumption or anything you can call it is always by always by extremely low cost. Craig so on your point extreme you've wunderkind Skok always look for X-Gene euphoric tyle with Wally because that's how my training plan works. All right.

A bicycle from 1988 and doubling up is pointing up to me that I can make good money. 92 88 means you can move higher and higher and Excel Tricare at 92 99. So it's a long effort. Now on the pie chart this is what you are seeing as the max profit now Max profit 19:00 want to sell 19:28. Trust me. Perfect. That's what I call the one of max profit. So this is the thing to note. Trust but profit is somewhere in the max profit. A good trade. So if you're creating an amount anywhere between one to two then it's what I call not bad not good because to pay plus on every trade if you're trading five takes then it's a big plus for those trials. Their profit is gone. So will give me some slack here. I mean no profit no loss and that's not good, that's extremely bad.

So always look at the spread picked by right here. Then you should be offering a higher price right. It should be filled with anything below but not extreme like a limit. Now you don't have to start Frank if it offers that opportunity then comes commission. So I would choose a broker that offers the least commission because for a day a commission is to be a problem. You cannot have X-Gene commissions now right here. It jumped up from 92 when I got to get the loan that took 21 Pipp candy. Now it tells us to buy on the top of the counter. But I have learned that waiting for a few falls off to get this right. If it doesn't I won't break. That's my rule. And if you look at it like I said to buy in, look up at nine to 16 and then get a cell signal right at non-guilty Toti to take a plus. So let's look at how much bigger the Canlis is if it is already giving it to anyone who profits from the lowest point. And it's not worth trying.

What is left in that trade to make money for you. It cannot make 100 percent profit on the five minute talk so don't expect that kind of profit and be vigilant now and again. Things are right here 93 22 and things feel right. 93 29 22 and 2:31 Pipp laughed. And then it falls off again again again again going lower and lower and lower. And now again I think by 92 1998 and it jumps back up to make a good deal of profit is Zic minus. Nope it's not wait you're right Kate is and men get in about 8 here at 92 and make sure to pay proper care as well. Doctors are to drop their profit but here we lost something. I believe 1982 and when Tampa lost and 24 picked me. Twenty one is profitable. Craig 7:37 and you had more straight games then because of the highest movement in price to disavow you make a plan B like this is the rule number one you should have an exit strategy.

And they think it should. They should not be blocked and how can it be blocked by having the volume at that time or having extremely good warning. So before starting trading just look at it, what's the average wall in the five minute take hours and locks that can create a thousand locks in for 10000 locks and you can take 100 lock reasons because the exit strategy of my plan makes money. But if your exec is blocked and you cannot exist at the exact price then my plan is telling you a quick exit up on 91. And you look at it up on 9 3 0 4 0 6 plus on the Sprint network break that Sprint because the basic assumption of this plan is that you can exit exit point 91 to exact path. Now if I'm looking at it right here close I ended up on 91 though.

But the next five minute gate open that night alone could open one pipe higher so you can easily expect two point ninety one. That's the basic assumption. And it should have so much training that let's say 10000 papers in five minutes. So you can sell it easily because it is enough to sell easily. You are not leveraged. Daim is nothing. The aim is to accept because the money will be made on all chalk either it's a five minute check or any other chart but you can easily accept as. So exciting is also an important part of taking. Now if you move further to sell, sell goes down. And now I'm buying it again. This is minus zero. This is bluster. So at this moment we'll be buying a 0.19 one pipe like me please.

And I can hear Sorry not to hear him. If we zoom in to price moves flat and suddenly open tire and it says sell right here 0.9 to the 2:04 Viborg to zero point ninety one five six to nine Pipp profit to always remember if you're trading on the five Majok then pennies idea profit and you can lose those pennies on the spread or on the commissions. So I'll just use a broker that has the lowest commission. Otherwise don't take five minutes because your profit is Maxton 12. She cannot lose a perp on the commission. This is one and it is like five that create nine five make is not for you because for you you're creating is extremely limited your profit and loss are based on the cost of creating if you're buying something at her dollar and owning one dollar and two cents then your profit margin is extremely limited. And this is trading so things can go bad as well.

Now profit is what a shopkeeper keeps and for a shopkeeper he's buying things on credit and he's not investing his own money. But here you are investing your own money so you're not investing it for two cents. So remember this and create intelligently. Money is going to be made. I'm showing you all here on shows like my quarters my needs easily be made. But the concept is to understand which things make money for you to understand that the biggest hurdle for a creator is commissions as charges on fees are all those fees. A big player doesn't trade with those fees for example. I mean often create that you people aren't being offered rates at extremely low. If you are offered at a rate at Hadar I'm being offered the same rate. I don't think so. I can get a huge amount at one percent of the cost and that true cost helps you make easy money.

So I am again telling you only if you are offered some kind of suck up shot or move to a high growth move to a deal which I don't think is great because I don't think to make money for your brokers right here. We bought it here at a point ninety six point ninety two to one now that run Pepp should be to your commissions and the special note picture so that you create a fact then I can easily make money for default font and prices back up to say by actually $0.90 or three. And what's the best spot? It looks to be a Double-O and a huge amount is coming your way. It tries as follows. And writers fault on deck for it to sell again one big profit.

So if you're creating five five minutes then you should have your cost associated with one pip so that you should know that you can exit at the same price within one PAIP problem. Now just look at it further here. It was 1984 and the next year it opened at the same price 93 raffle. So you can execute at the same rate and your commissions if they are below 1 Pipp extremely good because that's how you make money because all of you are paid the cost automatically and you are trading again and again and again and again. Now this is what I call the best thing. This was the first slow second Rotolo. It represents that huge sums of money is coming your way because the mortgage loans they make the higher the flight can be still pointing higher. Now it's going you're here at two point ninety two you sold your body take zero point ninety five plus for it I tell you.

Finally, crowding means extreme training. But the concept is to make you money. There will be fewer trades that will be extremely brutal and they will change your game plan. Now again expanding our So you can buy 8:51 but don't expect 5 weeks to give you huge sums of money. This is the game plan now 20 higher higher higher. So is that one trade that you would like to remove all our base. This is mynahs So we did here at 92 in 87 and exited here in 93 15. So it means to put profit in our previous state. If you remember we made a profit so it was covering its commissions. Say what it means it was like flat trading. And here we made that good profit and boom out. Now some of you might ask why on earth we go at such a big can we have two or six popping profit within this of something because it would go bad.

So if you have expectations of going higher to the brink of an end and it goes higher. So the headline will be moving up. So we have a like over for the Latas. This gap is our best friend. That we Anglicare in the Pennis example they are told not to enter. Let me show you that point right here. Eight or nine and close on the play Top Billing tells us not to enter if it were closed right as it did right here. That was not that dangerous but this is because one can last 20-25 Peppe. Now you cannot make more than 10-15 put on a regular five minute trade. So it means all the profit is gone. That in fact one can I am tied at the top right here. It makes sense to enter the quarter with a gap in between the price and doubling the ban doubling up and telling us that it feels like growth and stops then even our losses will be moot. But if it goes all our way then our profits will be extremely high and that's exactly what happened. Thank you.

USDJPY 1H Day Trading

Hi guys to me, they will discuss restoring the Japanese yen. For one hour Lee talked. Now as you can see I just clicked here and selected the two indicators that we are discussing in this Book. Now the thing to note you a strong Japanese yen is our day. These two countries are one of the most popular topics. And they're actively traded not to profitability chance on U.S. dollar Japanese yen Peyre are. I would like to say that the profitability chart is far easier than any of the four expect. And if you remember the lock and PAIP chapter that I discussed, a Japanese yen pair US dog gap is in your Pipp stock from 0.01 there's no four digit pickup number applying in U.S. or Japanese yen.

Chuck Now as you can see are buying stocks when they were MATV cross'd up and it goes till the highest moment in time on the MUTCD crossover. As you can see this was pretty high tech. Costco does seem approximately. Now one thing to note the broader crying as you know I've always discussed it and if you look at it the product is down. Not down bouncing like today, it's been down for the last many months. The highest high was done in July. Then there's August down and now it's September. Two months down. Now when you have such a down movement go first of all be concerned because you know profitability depends on your trading metric because before the start of trading you have to decide you are a buyer or you are a seller number one. But if you just focus on the trading plan it still makes you money even if you look at it right here. It's showing you a fall.

But if you just look at the buy sell order right tactic by acting on getting into any price and a sell was right. Wait a minute and then sell war on any loan 20. So you're never married or gained any money just like it happened to be by and happened to sell. So it was the flat trading you went on in the fall and that's what I wanted to show you. The decline is so good that even if you put in the wrong crowd then you want to let you have a laugh but not whenever they make CDs at extreme levels. Example right here. It's minus minus 0.02 4. That's huge. If I just zoom out. I will show you that if I mark a horizontal line on this low then the indices near the lows not near the highs and therefore as of now there's a high chance to make money because just look at it right here. Yes. First off I mean this is the second loss is really not the dollars are higher.

But—if he does approximate sorry the price is approximately flat. So it sort of brought him up. I counted in the eight or 109. Let me check. To buy. Order comes in here at 10 in 897. Then you could have easily made a profit off 109 47 that huge, that's a 50 page profit. So this shows you that even at a stock gnomic because I have just zoomed out and shown you that for three months it was pointing downward. So there was a hard cost to make money but you still made money even though the high was near the high. Still you had a 50 percent profit and a 50 per profit is exceptionally in forex trading and especially in day trading. Now let's move forward to see how the trading goes now as you can see the MSEE continues to fall. And that is Arlynn.

That's like the maximum mark that we made and even to the floor. So it means this at the lowest part of the fall. And as we discussed earlier the last part means the best part because any time that is exceptional highs then it means a change in trend number one. Number two they could be divergent as well. I don't know if that wouldn't exist. So you'll always be vigilant in buying or selling. However buying is usually EFI easier than selling because selling. Usually I don't buy a select number of people and therefore they are far more vulnerable because everyone is mine and that's the real risk. Now right here I can name so 91 you would have bought it. So let me market hundred into 91 minus minus we'll be selling price rises right. That's right.

But if you remember our name first it is for the top pulling back we don't expect the US to get anything to cross the bull toppling about the first is for all. It's all very clear once it crosses doubling up and then you start to like five more. But for a first attempt you know even the falling building. Now when they say even if you're not selling a damn you're just putting a conservative profit on it. You're not selling. You will be selling once doubling the bond goes down and does across or However as of now it's pointing up up and up. So you should be extremely bullish and right. Is there a crossover? No it's not. So you wait for another day or you find another out. And this is the quarter or so you would have bought it right here somewhere. Let me check.

Yes. Right. And you were so late. Let me bring it here. Now you bought it at 91 and you sold it at hundred and nine thirty. That's one dollar thirty nine. Sent in different but in Pip's. That's a 139 Pip. That's huge. Except it's still awesome. However there was a catch. Now as we discussed earlier, as a day trader you would be holding the next day. So you would have bought it here. I timed you to 91 and collegiate hunger seven eighty two. That's at approximately eight or nine per hour plus. Then the next take opens on doubling back. So you would never buy it here. You will wait for the closing here. Daniel by opening as you a hundred ninety eight. Thirty four. Let me market right here. Stocks to rise rise rise.

And again it said sell or you would be selling for like dates last trade here in 8:38 you boarded a time when needed. Twenty five. That's a 13 percent profit. This for the approximate 10 plus. So let's presume it's a breakeven trade till now. Then again you'll be buying the next day. At dope one hundred eight thirty nine. And the price runs up let me check yep the price runs up. Up up and up. And up. And this is the second last candidate of today. So you'll be selling it. So basically you made it from 1985 till handing in 93. That means a 100 profit now although from this moment till this moment it was 140 per profit. But as we enter a decade never goes for the next day.

Before he gets out and you would have got out right here and right here. So far stock you would have absolutely no profit no loss. But you always follow the trade till the end. And that's the reason I always show you to buy and sell of the doubt to buy and sell Mark because this is the tricky part. People get confused, don't you leave like last day hot whenever the price has jumped so much and they have not given money. So they simply sell, they say as hell or that you'll choose another stock or another for its option. But that's the key. Never lose your heart when you are in the trade. To trade because pulling up on an MSCE is your lifeline. If it was thin, it's a buy even though from Best Buy to this there were plenty when you had not made a single penny a single dime.

Still you would buy it here because the reason is you stole the trade. You don't create it. And most of our Japanese yen is so watertight that it's easier to make money. It has so much liquidity that it's easier to buy one. Phrixos how many 839 you can simply easily buy at 8:39. Is no problem that I like that. I mean just go beyond the seat and take the decision within ten seconds within five seconds. Your buying order window should be open day by day and that's like you have to be vigilant. You cannot leave the market and go away. That's the number one reason. So your training plan is so easy. You have made a 100 per profit without any problem. And the price then moved up.

But if you look at the embassy it hasn't given us a bicycle as of now. And once it gets right here the price crosses to cross and they're building a bank on top and that's the best thing for a trader off my plan. So 891 you'll be buying 981. And let's move forward. The price moves up up up back there though a problem or let's look at it from this week. This was the first time. And this is the second time now it was a bubbling band right. So it should have jumped higher but did not dare miss this point being that there is something wrong. Although the price is above them, the CD above is pulling a bond and pointing towards the best profit bucket thing to be vigilant and the gap between the blue and red line is Red used to exceptional moments now is it across or not.

So wait, is it a crossover now? Yes it is. So you all afternoon 10:17 right here. Now this is a day strike because this started at 5:00 a.m. and completed at 3:00 p.m. so you would deduct 10 17 Again 26 profit often within a day. That shows you the profit magnitude you are making money on each and every tree and ad like this last trade was the most dangerous one. Because if he was making a second low or high. Not a good sign. But still you made money. That's the power of the plan. Now it's a crossover on the downside. And as you know after it doubled up it usually means not a good trick but the price continues to tell you that it's not breaking and going bad. So I told you to be on your toes and to be a buyer again. And that's what happened here in 1935.

Now you might take the bullying them you haven't crossed it to cross or haven't happened. But whenever the price crosses the building a band and there's a smaller gap left then don't wait for the gap. Just buy it at ten thirty five. So we will be buying a place here for Aitkin and let's move forward. And here there is a crossover. So you sell something as simple as that. Now you sold it a tangent and fifty two hundred and fifty meant 15 typing profit. Not a bad trade. You're still making something out of it. And that's what proves that the plan is brilliant. And this is all within a day's trade. Now the MSEE continues to go lower. But just look at the price. It's not to go lower and dasht a Polish sign.

Now either you could have bought it here in downtown D1 or you would have boarded here. It's up to you but you will be buying it again. And so when do you want to? Because both the rates are the same. So. Hundred and ten 71 females for the dislocated MECC crossed up and then fell off. Now this is what I call a loss that I cannot avoid. You have to sell it by 10:56

and that's a loss. But this is what I call part of the trading at 10:56 is to sell. And it's a 15 year loss. So you made a 15 percent profit here and you lost 15 of profit here. So you are flat. But the question remains. Just look at the trading you are all lost in net profit your losses are extremely smaller and they're usually absorbed by the previous games.

And if you look at it you had previous gains that are exceptional profit a hundred Pipp profit and here we will make money in 981 and they sit down. So would the altar of profit. So we are going to be a tiny 30-35 per profit and use it to create our life and take care of ourselves. Now the price falls but the real risk now comes down. Just looking at it for the first time it has broken the building and going back creates a problem. However, if you want faith by you going to buy the human reason you mean that or when it breaks the building go back on the lower part. It doesn't mean that the Kenyan fortune will happen. Right. And it usually means a lot of rallies around the corner. So our use of their trust really as a day trader doesn't care about the longer term basis.

So your aim is to profit. I mean 6:52 as you are by Lake Mitri check it. No Hanun 10:43 is named 10:43. And let's check for the day Mythili crossed it up. Now if you look at it the gap between the blue and red line is starting to reduce. Not a good thing. And the crossover happened to you this year. No, it's right here on Dango. Now the thing to note again. But first let me put in I can and show you the talker profit in 10:43 110 86. So it's a 40% tape of profit in total but it's not for you. We'll have to see how that trade would have gone. That means you would have bought two. No, that's a new day. Complete profit would have come into your pocket because the day ended right here the previous day and this was a new day.

So you would have bought it and told it and made exceptional money without any problem for it to pip. Now you are 170 people profit. Excellent. Now it again rises up C and falls off. Now if you look at it right here it was a buy signal 18. And this is a hundred twenty five profit not backed so you can see that the plan will turn in everything and U.S. dollar Japanese yen Geely offers a far higher money making opportunity. And that's the reason I have added it in this book. Although initially in this book, the Japanese yen was not added, after I received so many queries. So when they request to add Japanese yen I have added and I must tell you it's one of the best I and I repeat it's one of the best for beer and the best for expect us to Orosius Frank to look out for that as well.

Now just to sum it up if I just threw out these are your traits. You started on the extreme low this blue line was extremely low and it has given you a good profit but if you look at it from the top the high is getting reduced which shows you that the number of profitability balls are numbered. So always check them out. They will help you understand what the future holds. If it is like you or if it's against you now I am telling you to buy buy buy all these signals. But I want to show you the long term current because the river changes its outlook. If it changes it's like. But don't you want it to signal before the change and these are the signals that we are destroying to give you and before you have to be always vigilant in that because one genius then it will be complete mayhem.

And if I go further it continues to rise up rise up rise up but if you look at it the price was right nine forty seven and 155 that took a profit in between what the highest high off the water and best for them are the highest high the low high. So that is a current shifting and this is the first time that it had broken the building. And this is the second time. So it gives you a complete picture of what the price is doing. And right here it's the third time. So we can see that slowly and gradually it is teaming its direction. But I am always told to leave by the buyer. Yes it's telling you that the dangers exist and dangers exist. But the question comes up: how can you easily make money? You always choose the easiest but by orders.

If you want a truck so I won't say don't charge so I will take you out shocked shell sell. Remember that at that time sharks were numbered but not so many people. He went on to head for any community. Not every hedge fund is happy with chalk selling. So the old numbered people are backed in by those in charge. And with my order like my plan you can even make money and won't you'll have money in your pocket. You are creating capability to automatically improve docs to take paying How ever or keep your hand on the pulse of the market to understand what you're doing. Now the highs we're getting to. So it's a step down due to the bucket problem. You want to change your plan, you will stick to it. I'm listening. You see a major part going down. So this is rule number one. If you have any questions, bosomy from the Q&A session to.

USDJPY 30M Trading - Risk Management

Hi guys to pay because you will start a tap which means you can chalk and discharge two minute chocolate. So basically you are using your own money during the day because that's what day trading is. Now as you have gone to the food court you are seeing that I'm discussing two different types of Goch and sometimes even more. Now basically I'm trading you know where do you start now. Are you talking for like a few hours to 10 days? So as a trader you squared off by the day and by then actually opened. Now that's a bit tricky as well as something for a person to be alert every day and to follow the game every day. Then comes the 30 minute chart. Now 30 minutes Jack doesn't offer the same kind of flick profitability as Chuck.

But it comes to Doley chalk yearningly the day is easily squared that day. So you don't need to worry about whether the next day's open or closed. You're a buddy and told him to come back here which would have been profitable or you would have been here at one time and so the day care went full. However the concept that I'm trying to discuss here is that trade is within a day best great day. Example this trade you would have balked at one of 868. Now this trade would have to be stopped right here because the case closed. And open the next day. So they stayed on the back their opportunity then went out to check the Like possibility of removing the open toes probably an error. It could not offer the same kind of investment as one hour each week.

Now you can also find a chart that I've discussed extensively in this court. However, a five minute chart is extremely fast. You need to create again and again and again and at extremely fast paced. And many of my students have told me that they are not happy with them. So what's the solution now? I would ask the question: where do you think it's best? NOLAN I really talked to one trader. So it's just fine. And then just following it at the end of the day you just sell the next opening you just buy. It's like what I call blind trading. You don't need to do anything special. And as you are not taking so many decisions. So it's like easy trade. It doesn't affect your personality. Now on the flip side a 30 minute embolden me to trade. Now the example I just mentioned here. This is a one day trial.

This is like any other trade craft trading and trading for. So it's like every day trading however and I'm repeating it will be somebody with me having losses. Now all the talk is like a distinct possibility because your exchange could do it. So you have a better opportunity to make money. Know on the chart could be like. He would have lost a few cents every day. And usually people don't like to lose. So if you're one of them that turns the chalk in front of parents rather than being faster or slower now really than toting the chalk is best for you you know as I discussed with you whenever Tony said he makes a Double-O. There's a higher chance it will offer you far more money.

Now if you would have back right to one who is 9:29 you would have sold out to one 1 and 26 46 that would have meant 17 texts. Now that's not a big deal but that's not 17:10 Dec. 17 Pip's which means an awesome route on a simply awesome again because you are trading day trading. Expect 100 percent gain. Now add to what I call cooking like money making wine. This can be what's called my child. It makes so much money that it can make money. However, you are seeing up close as well again. It's the first low or the second they're offering you a pastry to inherit. So Ben is always looking out to see what is happening now as you can see from zooming up that the price was in your face for now before the free fall. We've had many meetings to take net long term transactions.

The full cost was fifty point one and a loss fifty seven point five. Then gainings just chill production which was low monthly report and so on and so forth. So the point is after all this news the price fell off you're right. However, let's look at it right here. Lousteau was matched here not close to matching. So a team is coming this high. The highest high was matching this high. So this is how you understand the long term goals. Now it's in a freefall as it is right here. And I would tell you that your profit making machine won't be giving you an exceptional profit. Example Herc's 110 74. And here it is 110 ninety six point six. Our purpose had a very low window. But here it goes. And intent. So when t this log Yeah it's just thirty five cent or 25 plus.

So at the end of the day you just need to get on with it because basically this is how the trading plan goes. You will have some days of losses and some days of exceptional profits and the like. Good point to choose from the daily chart. It fits in a free fall or you know like good up crying because basically it's easier to make money on an upgrade and it's not easy to make money and downgrade. I'm even discussing downgrading because I want to assure you that even in the fall you'll meet 20- 25 cents. And he lost 30- 35 cents. So sick when he had 10 plus. Right. You would have said by text 5. And the price would be 10- 12. That would have again meant 20 Pip maybe check or going down to old.

Thirty five. Yep going to. It's like today 25 five plus inches by hugging 994. And so I didn't like the fact that it was 70 plus times. I can get ninety five and sell right corner 9 to the ticket plus However what I'm trying to tell you is something really important. I am trying to kill you when you see a print fall that has it's breaking you know putting a band on the downside. It's not breaking the building of a banner on the top side as you have like Till now you have a team in the private sector where I showed you how it goes up and makes him money. Now that something is understandable that it goes beyond billing and it makes you money. But if it's painting the penis close to doubling up and now how do you know that that's a bad credit and now should not be buying. You should be shocked at selling or staying outside the market.

Because that's a good question. If you don't know you won't be in a good position now here you can see approximately 100 piping total losses. From here because this is where you start making money again and when you age 68 is like we see 68 is the buying point and I mean 69 is selling things with any money. They said that in 84. And this is a 95 to cut best profit. So basically you would have lost approximately 100 back from here 20 seconds when you tell her queen. Jacqui now the question comes up how to solve this problem because basically as a day trader you should have a backup plan for all kinds of problems. Now the thing to note is always remember that doublers on the MSEE side back up past Frank D'Albert high on your MSCE side are your worst enemy.

If you look at it as I went out and am now zooming out farther now I just look at it right here. It's called Double-O. This is a complete bottom low so that like you know that way I would tell you to make money although the price you see is going straight it's not doing anything but a moving price. Your kid doesn't get you except in lotus. It's what I call not actually number one. Number two: how do you know when not to buy? Because I have been telling this quote for a long time. Now if you follow a long time you won't have this issue because the long term will be saying. So be out and you won't have that problem. But how big bear lake that game from the incredible Chakiris fell yes you can go into the longer term though and understand the market and act accordingly. But the market gives you signal number one.

Just look at the price. What is the pricing here? Thirteen hundred twelve hundred eleven hundred eleven hundred eleven hundred nine. So the highs continue to go lower. You it's starting to grow up. It's now breaking the PSII So I remember what if it peaked to highs. Good for you. If it doesn't then there's something wrong. Number one true number two lows now on the below. Let's look at it from here. You would have bought 27 alone. So Nick 11:27 again back here at 10:00. Sixty three hundred twenty seven. So five plus. Now how do you like to solve this problem of losses? From Damon the entry and the answer lies in seeing the price itself. If you're just joining in and that mattered when I showed you losses I'm showing you that the price is not walking on the upside. It's going down. You have a minute thing right here.

It's not only like on a free fall breaking the pianist playing a band but it's not moving up now only to remember if you like to remember the play. Understanding go. Like you I told you when ever the red line the price is falling dragline act as if he just didn't blow. And that's exactly what is happening. It's Dr. Dragline here, here , here and here. So the question comes up: how do you create now? My answer to you is first of all only make mistakes with the least resistance and that is done by seeing the pudding about the band being contracted. That's a good thing for you isn't it offers you like. And that this will go bang. If you're wondering if the press got it bad. Craig Dapo the band act you are a polemic for the public. The best thing for buyers. However my band almost looks down.

Just look at it right here. It's looking down looking down and it's not contracting by compacting. I mean something like pulling a band is contracting right. And the price is going straight. It's not falling or breaking the law brewing up at work here here here. Why on earth did we get a break on the loose. So if you see something like this don't create a not only losing a member then ever toppling a bank breaks the top example. Let me show you right Ted. All right. And the price of stock fell off and just for straight trading please stop. And then you peel off. But the concept is perfect. And then if you would have bought. I mean 10:42 and started here in 1976 that would have meant to keep number one number two.

Now just to summarize number one fan who expects not to play a band and you can play Pentair if you see a price falling and breaking a bank and out Wakeford the crossing on the highest building up and once he does all that it's like too late. All right. So wait until this fall. So right here and right here you could anchor right here. You couldn't do it. My point is you have to stay out number one. Number two if you're a member the risk manager Mike chapter I told you all stuff if you're not following your game plan then you have to put applauses not docketed number one do. That means if you were out of pocket at any loan twenty six and the price was just the highest point and you started to fall off then you have to put a stop loss to get out.

You cannot risk everything. You have to be vigilant. You have to be strong enough to get out at no profit no loss. Now these are important things. Reason being whenever the market is going with you you won't have to blink and you won't have to really risk management techniques because the price is like jumping higher and higher. However if it doesn't go to your end you have to have a game plan. You cannot be a naive example. I don't know who to buy right to act in 1980 right now the price went up 110 90s the highest point in 1982 is the highest point in and then it fell off. It fell off and broke the previous close and made 1965 that close to 10 again it fell off and made up one in 10:54. Now at the last point it's going down 58.

If I just I mean I would be able to clearly show you that this is saying by right here 1980. Right. However it does directly and starts to fall off and best to list pulling up and right here. If I just a moment ago showed you right here just pulling the bank on the lower side. Now my point of view is it tried to go up again and stopped at the red line. When you see something like this please be vigilant. Crank it up even if you run into your lowest point like this thing can and should act and stop loss. Now I am in the Stop-Loss only and I'm debating only when the price is on the play. It's breaking the lowest pulling the back. It's not breaking the highest pulling back when he does that. You have to be like waking DeGroot you cannot trade just like that.

You have to have roots. And that's the number one rule. See it. The lowest pulling a bag when it was breaking up purpling up and then your problems won't be that much if you would have bought it next a hair 1982 tourist was Vidler the price fell off broke. No, it came back up and then it started to go down right here. So my point of view was to understand the game. If it falls off and rises up and then again falls off that's not a good sign. Try to get out on the next rise up. If not then anyone looks at your price and doubles up and contract your price comes on the blink of an that's not a good thing because above doubling again that's a pretty good thing. If the price goes above back if your price goes on or above to abandon the price has plummeted and that's a real problem.

This is the loaning game you can knock. I repeat you cannot make trading in such a situation. I would suggest you do get out. The reason the price should have gone up. It's not stopping here. Not a groupthink. It opened higher and linked to your article. The price should have gone up. It didn't. It should have gone out prior to your dating and now falling. So it's telling you to be vigilant whenever you see something confusing you get out. And I repeat. Captain he has an all Bustamante like a first thing in any trading in your own capital. If you're buying and the price is not acting good then get out. Yes you might lose the money making great no problem but you have to take care of the money first thank you.

USDJPY 5M Day Trading

Hi guys to take a five minute chart as a five minute job to something that 50 percent of gay Curtis love. Now I'm choosing five in chalk on the X-Gene lowest level . Today it's showing is 15 February and today is considered a date. Today is 1933. Now if you look at it right here it told you to buy a time in 6:36 and told you to sell 806 1:54 doctor could expect profit. Right. But if you look at this end it gives you new ones at that time. You usually must please help but only those who remember what a crane is. If you look at five o'clock it's showing the trend was lower and the trend was falling. It was breaking previous lows. My dear Bollinger Band is going straight everywhere. Before that it was falling off.

So the first thing in a trading situation is understanding the clock if it will, like Publish or Perish because then the plan can give you the most amount of money in a fall. It can stop the fall. It can make it like 10 percent on it or fall it can extremely like limit your losses. But you're not creating lots of trading to make money. So first of all your game plan is to choose a good stock. Our fire expert and Dan Craig, now a five minute chart, didn't expect a huge amount of money before. If you're out of pocket here at 609 the crossover would whatever happened year time in 6 06. That's an exceptional fall before the last 10 minutes. See it's an exemplary fall now in a five minute chalk you feel it and the price is moving straight straight straight.

You are buying at faults that still like magnitude time. A five minute Cluedo won't have time to make a decision because it was at such a pace. But if you remember to ask the management chapter you have to have a Stop-Loss placed. I always remember as a band contract your archtop losses or to get a higher post here. Talk to us here. No one said the price was going straight up and contracted. So your price was all too low. Don't dislike it. Contracted again. Now if it contracted I mean. So we won't be encouraging a stop loss to DENSELOW because it's extremely hard to price. We will be sticking to guns to stop loss. I'm fine and next year. So once it started to fall off undisclosed Stop-Loss could have got hit 6 0 9. I'm very glad you brought it.

Wanted it to come in six or nine. Plus would have been your buying price and there were no losses. Now you might ask me why it would be good for this fall season. The reason is whenever your bite rate was like a momentary tickle not only does a five minute count and it might be maximum. And I really can't like all this time. But the point is these are only candles that can be an important break. So whenever so much time costs and the price falls after that then you should not be at a loss because so much time is wasted. So your losses should not be there. The tempo is set right here at tonight and 6:17 it costs rose rose rose rose past and when it fell off. Now again no budget at 670 right here on this good in Canada.

The price goes up. Fell off. So this fall, this is kind of low. And then Yukawa's vaca now you should have a stop loss because you could have a stop loss right here or here. It's up to you but you should have a stop loss that you didn't because in a five minute chat the trading is so fast. And in that fastness it takes time to understand what's happening. So rather than vaping for the crossover to happen sometimes you have to hit your stop loss because at the end of the day Stop-Loss is made so that you don't lose much money because of the Pinelands scanner. So that buys a time and takes 10 bucks from here is that comment takes 15. So showing your buyers that come into 6 17 and this fall or lower.

Here's how 9:6 15. So it means a. Yes if out of it and the Sharpless has placed Optik the price has gone up because then you will know that this was the fall before that. You know this was a foreigner not so after that you have placed a stop loss here. If the price falls at such a fourth as it did and you would have placed numerous stop losses then you would have to scale it here. I commuted 6 16. Now this doesn't look so bad. This 406 15 discovery is 660 so one or one sank. It's not like that. Biggest problem is it. No it's not. But the concept is that you're in a five minute chart. It's too fast. So you have to trade before the fall. You have to be vigilant. Just look at how it fell off but such a force. Now if you stopped last exploding you would have a kid who turned 6 12 now your stop loss would have been here.

I had to take CO_2 only to sell here at 8:34 and you buy 160000 trucks on your tape plus not a big loss but to top it off, if the Bible is not here you'll buy it once here. Then you would have to place the stop loss because if somehow you cannot sell on the crossover then you have to sell on the low because if you won't it will be falling off within the next 15 minutes to an extreme lowest level. And you can't really be wiped off so creating in any plan trading in any place trading on any chaulk requires you to place a stop last season because at the end of the day your first aim is to stay in the market. You've seen industrial volume Of course that my plan books. It doesn't have any problem. So if the plan works money will eventually come out. That's not a problem.

The problem is D's fault because if you let you know you sold under cross or somehow you missed it and you'd never had to stop loss. Somehow you missed it in the fall. Your body hears it. 6:12 and Louis Lora's hundred fifty six. That's a huge 60 plus. Now you're actually in a $5 check on your last one to keep it up. So 56 plus means and two more are 20 times more. And that's huge. That's exceptional. So if you're planning an anti-gay trade or have this information ready Stop-Loss is already gross or sell already. You can not sleep on it. Symbols that even if you're sleeping you should have a plan placed example Stop-Loss is so that you don't lose more than a certain limited amount.

If it does then that's a big risk. Then the price rises up again and it says by right here at hand good in 571 and here I go iron 571 prices moving higher higher higher and higher. And if you look at it you bought it here. So this was the Lousteau just for the Stop-Loss. Then the price moved higher. So if you would have lost your lost to this level now to this low now is for the lowest low first. This is the second lowest. So now your Stop-Loss has increased. But even with this increase it's not on your buy price. And here it's a crossover. So you would be simply selling it here. You bought it here at high gain Piscean do on until late here. Kenyon 577 a six day profit 02 that's not a huge profit but it's a good profit.

It is a profit to first TINC. Remember if you lose and you go trade in profit then eventually you'll have a big profit. So the first aim in any trading decision in any job is to be in profit. Now is it a crossover idea? Yes, right. It's across our 591 plus to licks I can put and I can hear Dan let me put in. I'm going to buy it right here and 591 and the price moves straight straight straight straight straight up and does across all where I go out in between buy and sell. You still need money. 591 sorry we do meet and hang in 598. Again sound profit. Now profit every time is a brilliant thing. It tells you that you're on the right track.

That's what I'm trying to tell you. Good profits will always follow because your game plan is so good. The only thing to note is putting a stop loss because if the price moves against you you have to have a way out to see what happens. But whenever it is such a fast straight five minutes you'll have to be vigilant to get out even on the hourly chart. I suggest calling to place a stop loss. You run on the hourly chart although the hourly chart is not as fast as five minute crazy but still I suggest and if you look at it it's a sell. And here again Crofter when you would have bought it. And is it a good buy because it's Grotzinger pulling a bunch and cutting a bit longer than means to best buy. So you would have bought it here for $296 Dean and it moved higher and higher and it tells a sell right here this fall on your 6:12.

This was 186 Todi once in close but not a Bacary reason because as of now your profitability is usually 6 7 cent 6 7 pips. So rent plus isn't that bad. They'd move higher again and here you would have wanted to hang 625 however. Now it's far more dangerous. Reason because the next day open is lower than it was in the. It does this. This is what I call the riskiest moment ever. However stick to your game plan and wait now and move down and then it starts to move up. So you know it's going on your crack. You wait however you'll buy here at home your 625 is still vulnerable because it's only for profit. It's not a huge amount. It goes straight straight.

And is this across or. Yes it is. So you sell through a profit again. This might not look to you as a big profit but my concept is it's not about the big or small profit. It never was. It will be. My point is always to stay in the groove. You'll find one group Craig that will change everything and to get that one good. You have to play again and again as a day trader trading again and again. It's not a problem you are today who wants to create again. So that's not a problem. A think that might have a problem with it being broken large huge sums of money that they created. This is not his problem. He likes to give his broker more money but he needs to be vigilant. He needs to be extra like what I call extra careful. He needs to sell every second. When you worked for yourself right. The next two seconds would have meant sell.

He cannot wait because if he would have then within 15 minutes his price was 806 and he had his last and now gone 200 625 and within 15 minutes it's gone down 200 6:16 and it doesn't look nice. Beyond doc so the price is moving straight. See Gheen nearest point to like. But it didn't get crossed. No it fell off. Now it is like a crossbow where I do. Yes it is. So I connect at 6:26. You will be a key. Wait a minute this is here. Let's move here. 6:26 musar is still here. 26:28 I bet you still need a stupid profit Kurt because at the end of the day if you keep on earning money that will help you in covering the future losses. Because always remember the trading plan you're trading could make money.

And that money will eventually go to Yosses that might exist in the future. But if you stop losses then those losses will be extremely small and then your net profit will be extremely large because as per my plan if you make a dollar and you lost 30 pips or 30 cent then you are still in net profits 70 cents. But if you implement Midas management techniques then those fall off 20 cents or 30 pax Melbourne to 15 Pipp So your profit rather than 10 percent will increase to 85 percent. So that's a 20 percent increase and that's a rejection of 50 percent in the losses. This is really important for a day trader because he is trading at an extremely fast market and he cannot risk so much money that the seat fell off. But such a force if you somehow would have not sold it here 628 and you would have got crushed here. In five nights.

So this is what I call the learning process. These are the by thing I mean takes zero or two but you will be placing a Stop-Loss like a place to buy first high you two you'll be placing the Stop-Loss here on the last your first to price moves higher once it moves higher. You'll be increasing the stop loss from this point till this point isn't good, not because the prices are very high. Why should I be putting the straw here and the polling is it's all coming back up. It is coming back up. Then my last if my stop loss has exploded telling about it should. Probably it should be higher. It should be on or below but not such a gap.

So if you're finding this low place it is where ShopHouse will increase. But now real profits are already far higher. To stop loss might not get hit. The question is if the fall can come at any time. So you have to be vigilant now. You are here. Knowing you do, you should look to fall for them and you pay a profit even though it fell off at such a force that he'd like most of the profits that you had already earned. Baghdad's fortified McReady Yes you can do anything about it. But the point is to be vigilant. Yes Stop-Loss is here. Moves higher again. And here is the thing to tell it. No it's not. It is a thing by reading you're saying buy right here. I 6:12 So you buy again at 6:12. And if you look at it all my Kriti you haven't seen me lose more than one pip one sink.

This brings to the question that a trading plan is so good. However I repeat DO keep stop losses. We're going to help you from the worst mistake ever. A falling knife is a falling knife kind of a market. Now here your blog your hair a tongue and 6:12 and toilet hair and 6:29 means sounding Bips profit exceptional. And if you look at it all it could have given us profit. And how many that have been we have been creating this is 16th Candice's or they'll succeed. So within a day you would have Beag take five profit without any doubt and your loss of that extremely limited only requirement is to stay put. You don't need to get Mahdi's, you have lost all Plus's you can trade without stop losses.

Otherwise it's the easiest plan ever money making machine back you cannot you cannot trade without stop losses. Yes you might be left at the lowest point and you might be trading at the highest point but you have to take the job losses no matter what the reason because it's an extremely fast market five Minick markets and this kind of dog can give you too much loss. It might take them to rule number one is not to fall into the trap of so much losses as our plan itself is so good that it will give us exceptional profit. So why take unnecessary risks? Thank you.

What is Short Selling?

What is shocking is that the most important question of all now shot telling is a seal of security. Our financial instrument is not owned by the seller. In other words it is borrowed from the broker. So you are borrowing it to sell on the market now shock selling is done with the belief that this doc is fonix-like will decline. Do want to go up. It's your belief and that belief is hoping to invest to buy like get back on the fall and make huge profits. So basically if you're buying anything you're buying it first and selling it later. But in a short sell you're selling it first and buying it later. So at the end of the day both buy and short selling trade looks the same but to buy trade is buy first sell later and short sell trade is sell first later. Now short sell can be done as a speculation on as a hedge against downside risk for a long position.

Example you own a hundred thousand shares and you believe that the market will fall 10 percent and then when you guys 30 percent up. So before the fall you can simply sell it off and buy it like putting up a put option. And once it reaches your 10 percent like all you buy a call option and basically both options cancel them out and you still own the Security number one. Number two is short selling it completely. Once it falls back you buy this cookie again and own the profit on the rights. Now short selling risks to risk and short selling is too radically finite and therefore short selling should only be used by expedient traders. Now in this book I tell you each and everything that every experienced trader knows. So you are like equipped with all the weapons now. This Book is a bit complex.

You'll be seeing much deeper indicators on the chart which will be telling you my postings at exact time. At the same time you will be seeing words like tons of information in one chalk and you'll be deciding what to do next. Accordingly, it will be hard for you but at the end of the day. You will become an experienced trader. Number one thing number two now is to say that the risk is finite. What do I mean? Now if you buy a stock at $10 and it falls off then what can it fall off to do to me to regularly lose $10 Max. You're going to lose more than that. But in a shark tale if you're selling it to a hundred then if it goes against you then it can go to a thousand dollars as well. So that is the risk part but the real solution to this is you should have a plan Plan A Plan B Plan C..

So if it fails to plan a dent and it goes to plan B you simply sell. And before you reduce your risk accordingly. Because in a buy you basically sit for like hold your life. It's like expecting it to come back in a short sale. This is not true. The rule is if it goes against you you simply sell your book a lot and you wait for the next go in trade. And that is again a short sell. So basically if you look at a thousand and it goes to 1010. It's a $10 loss but then you can wait and at eleven dollars you can simply short sell it again to make that money back. The losses back experienced traders are those that can follow their plan and before they can handle the risk accordingly. It's so easy and discord will prove that. Now how is chalk selling done as an investor?

JP G.L. a company trading at $100. Fall in price. You're expecting that Tefal you borrow and shock sell hand-brake shares a day later Campi Gildea pillocks bad results and the stock falls to 80. You simply buy just—and profit because you shock sold at 100 you're back at 80 to 20 dollar profit. Easy money and to cover your risk you can simply buy a put option. I'll put a stop loss as simple as that. No problem at all. That is what is short selling. Thank you.

Short Sale Metrics

Shot killed Max. Now all of the most popular metrics used to crack short selling are short increases and short interest ratios now shock interest means total number of years so short as a percentage of total company outstanding shows. So if they like let's say a million outstanding shows and a hundred thousand shares are sold. So it could simply tell you that 800000 shares are sold and as a percentage it will tell you 10 percent right shot increase stress means Bertold number of sharks all shared divided by stock average trading volume. Now this is really different now. And first I told you that 10 percent of the companies are tickets. Now usually it never goes that far. So it will always show you 0.2 percent 0.4 percent or so and like in short interest it tells you.

And you can see the complete picture but it's not really complete. Why? Because if one percent shares are a third and suddenly the market comes back then you cannot buy those 1 percent chock full shares on the day. It will take many days because 1 percent of the company's outstanding shares sold cannot be squared on the same day. So that's the risk that you can take. Karnit but in the short interest ratio it's simple for you because it's basically dividing those cheers by the daily average trading volume. So if the daily average trading volume is a hundred thousand shirts and let's see twenty thousand shares that's totally shocking to read you will know that if the market suddenly comes around then certainly 30000 by orders can come in and that can create a mad rush for the price to go up. So basically you will be seeing a stock that has to balance it out because bounce is really needed. A stock that high short interest is short in just is considered to be at risk of short squeeze. And it is done.

Eight out of 10 times the short squeeze. Now what is a short squeeze? Now I create a lock to basically look at the stocks with my interest or shark interest rate you know once I look at it and I find a short squeeze then I squeeze them. What does this mean? This means that I look at a stock which has let's say a hundred thousand shares traded energy. And once I see a short interest ratio of let's say 20 percent or 80 percent or something according to a share if it is not like a renowned company and doesn't have so much bad news I see a high short interest ratio then how do I squeeze. I simply put in more buyers. And once it crosses there like Stop-Loss metric are there action Stop-Loss Mattrick then they simply panic and once they panic suddenly huge sums of buy are coming.

And if let's say I bought it at $10 and I made the price from 212, I got it and then the shock sellers panic so they will buy it out. Now once they are buying they wouldn't be buying at 12th. They'll be making the price run. So basically I squeezed a stock. I bought more buy orders than usual. They used to come in at eight hundred thousand shares traded. So I simply put in a hundred thousand kids by my own account. So basically the first turnover was D'Albert because 100 years meant that all the common retail investors were buying and selling. So that's how that was told in church. But if I. On the one hand I want to do all the shows by myself so that makes Hitler 200000 thousand shirts once it makes 200000. Then it's suddenly a shock squeeze. Why?

Because once I get told that you're scum then everyone in the beginning was Joe who hasn't shorted any out. Our next mystery investor who hasn't been shocked sold it to look OK. Buying is coming. So it must be something extra. There must be some great inside news deals to come in. So from my hundred thousand shares it comes to an end 50000 shares by Once the price crosses like say from 10 to 11. Shock sells panic. They see huge buying and Delta panics a deal to come in to buy. So now from 150000 shares being bought it comes to 200000 chairs being booked and the price from 10 or 11 goes to 13 or 14. And short sellers are losing money. So they are simply like bidding it high and Wasdale bidding it high.

So I am selling my shares to them for being balked one step right out to gawk falls again. Don to always remember the short interest ratios should not be extremely high. Now when I told you that our buying up lexia 100000 cheered our daily credit I put a thousand shares. Now how do you alert your eyes when you do that? I analyze it by seeing the stock. If the short interest ratio is too high let's say 20 percent. That means that if the stock goes out of the window then those people who have short sold will be stuck. So all those look for it if it is a renowned company then Usually this doesn't come in because in every renowned company everyone is like a big. Now if s I R S I r I at a high number.

Dan daks stock should not be shorted as another manipulation by broker is to call in shock like shock possible. What does this mean? Shock possible. It means what the broker does is that I'm a broker and I see that SIRC shoes are getting higher and everyone believes that the price will fall because that's usually the reason. And so your numbers are getting higher. So what I will simply do is I'll simply call them up and tell them that I cannot play part of the shirt with x y z reason and Yunior squaring off. So what am I doing? I am making them by and one step by which I get paid commission and I simply allow the other let's say my client to short sell it.

So basically I doubled my commission rate by allowing the first investors to square by saying that economically Kubo and by allowing a third in which to chart Selek again I'm doubling my commission that A's and never when you politician now the shuttle is configured to be evil but it helps market it by order on the fall when no one is buying. Because if you see a stock fall 40 percent when you go to buy no you won't but a shot teller with because he is calculating his profit so his buy order is not to buy his buy order is just to square and his pie order act as a way out for a common investor who wants to get out of their stock. So therefore short selling is not that.

Now I know you might be like con. You might be extremely shocked to know this information that I mean brokers manipulate shock interest rates and stuff like that. But don't we usually stay in like good stocks that tech now brokers manipulate stocks that are not Crinan stocks that are extremely illiquid should never ever short sell an extremely illiquid Schrock. What does that mean? Don't sell a stock that have more than a hundred thousand shares still evil deeds simple stack if it's like volume falls below 400000 back to bad stock because if you have short term curve then you know a hundred thousand carries it to 1 percent now you as a retail investor should never be in a percentage don't. You should always be in like 0.01 percent. So all this type of shock is a stock with a higher volume. As simple as that.

A stock with a higher volume cannot be manipulated by brokers. And a short squeeze example if I'm looking at the shocks. I don't look at a stock that has a higher value because if it has a let's say 5 million shares volume or 1 million shares volume then I can squeeze it out. It's too many shares and too many shares means too much money involved that's too much risk from my end. So I don't take that risk and therefore no one takes Duckery even the hedge funds. We all look at stocks and if we want to short squeeze Trotsky's record stocks, not the stock that is extremely liquid. We've been warned to be thinking about Apple. Hope it's not possible and all the shock is painful. So an extremely good stock. And you want to look at all these risk metrics and that's what is shocking to somatics. Thank you.

Sources of short interest data

Hi guys. Now this chapter is really important for you. Why? Because like you really tell you how to understand what is happening in terms of chalk sales. Now I just say that a normal person will tell Apple about the shock in profit and then at Nasdaq. Now you can put any exchange you like when you put it in. It will show you a link. Example this one will show us the short interest in Apple. Where did it go? Heritage. Now if you look at it closely it's showing you to come to little details about the sheer volume, the short crust and days to color usually people Coate in 1.5 two days. That's one and a half days right here. They were using two days to delve into that apple. What is the short interest and what is the daily like for sheer volume average share. Kurts average daily sheer volume is 25 million chairs in desks like mandate in 11.

That is November 15. It was 31 million. And if you look at chart interest here on twenty five million it was 39 million and here it was 42 million. So it tells you what is really happening. And it helps you understand everything. Example: When it is shocking just how big it botched 12 months and a bit twice a month. So every month you're seeing it. What is available like a shock cell volume. Now if you look at it it's during Apple hospitality right now I have simply no idea what that company like makes money or not. I have no idea. But it is still showing its shark interest. Gratiot Now this company is usually a short squeeze target it can become a short quick target by looking at what is the average deal evolving.

This dog doesn't have a shock cell. Now let's move to any of the stocks. I remember I say Gee as a stock YASID with Kulas or even Google. Here you go. You can simply put any stock you like and see it short sell and trust. Example for Google it's coming up and if you look at it they have like a shock so shocking and just complete flake stuff and you can even get the latest news. Now this page does not support NYC and Amec stocks so it also helps you understand where the stock has really been created if we move back and just remove that. Now this is another great Website to focus our short squeeze dotcom. You should also be using this website. I use it a lot. Now it shows you daily squeeze ranking short interest, the short interest ratio that is gaze to cower. Usually it takes two to four days.

Shock percentage or float. Feet. Yes. Twenty point seventy two percent shot percentage increase or decrease it's decreased 7 percent short interest shares like short prior to today it was 14 million. Now just 13 million shares floated, 55 million total. That's a huge shock again this year. William today's only one point six million and trading volume averages only 5.5 million. So if you look at it this is huge. Owned by institutional investors it's like a ninety five point five percent good company. I buy shares for price to earnings ratio 23. But that is the point. It helps you understand what is happening. How many shares are shocked now. You might ask me. This is a group target not for Trotsky's. I would say no. Why? Because it's down by 35 percent now it might come back up but if you look at the tools that we discussed those tools will help you to understand what is coming up now.

If it is coming up a carney good my dude then I can see Michigan's shock squeeze into stock but that is only for a limited time period. I shortened it for many days, maybe two to 2.4 days. That's the max I can do. So this is how you learn them. Example: This is Google. Here you go. Average Joe oleum shocked interest days to coureur usually three days 2.4 nine days two point eight million shot sold. Average daily share volume was 1.2 million. So this is how you learn which year it is the most vulnerable. And I feel you know about Google. Google won't show you this. It will tell you it's rising higher and higher. And you can take a Google to Shortall now which if you will to know.

But once you will go to this book you'll find that group or even will allow you some days to shock, tell and make money. So there is no stock that says it cannot be chock full. But yes the stocks that are examples Hignett jewelers will make you more money because it's not a renowned name but Google won't let you make more money but it can be shocking. It can allow you to make money but not like tons of money but still you can make money. So it's up to you Rich doc to pick. But the point is to understand what really is happening. To understand if the short interest is increasing or decreasing because that's how you will understand what to do next.

What is Fibonacci Retracement?

Hi guys today we will discuss Fibonacci. My dad is what is Fibonacci retracement now Fibonacci to create works on an idea that market or loss falls below a certain limit and then moves to work to train regional people, not Chrisman . Placa is going to X-Gene to train. There is extreme high and extreme low. It could be like in a shorter move or in a longer move Leti on Mutley chalked or on an hourly chaulk. Now zero percent is considered to be the starting point for treatment that is Leti at the start of the fall and hundred percent is complete reversal of the artist. That is if it takes 100 percent mark down and like goes below that then you are sure that you're to complete your. And the market may not come back to its origin.

Now once you Plock Fibonacci crazy means it automatically places and frankly supports and resistance levels. Example at 20 percent thirty eight point two percent 50 percent. Half of to fall are sixty one point eight percent and then the last eight hundred percent. This tool helps identify stop loss Cleland's or Dogood prices to help Graydon's be as ready for the fall. Now this is really important because if you usually put in stop losses and I know that many of you are totally confused on tootling to price to fill Banaji label can help you with that now Fibonacci good treatment gives static limits and cannot change. So it's like a fixed deal. You can please tell Kancil daughter and it will work with Fibonacci retracement and that is what is not a race. Thank you.

Fibonacci Retracement in Detail

Hi guys today we will discuss Fibonacci retracement and I will help you understand how Fibonacci retracement is so powerful. Now for Fibonacci retracement you need to like pick and high and low if you need to understand what the limits are on top. Then you need to pick the highest angles if you need to understand what the lake levels are on the lower side. In the fall then you meet a low and high. So it's simple : you want to make an indicator and you pick a high and you pick a piccolo. And I've just made all them right here you go too far my it extends right now x 10 lines will be like extended forward. Just extended. What don't you see? You see that from too slow the first holes with this to price stock at that level.

The second level was. The price on the clothing basis never got up even on the do when it got up right here. If I just assume it, yeah right like closed higher. But the next day it opened the door and came below the line. It should not have come below the line. And this was the time it closed up but the next day we liked the correct time and it fell off. Then it goes back up again. Then again it made Eric Cantor. But as you can see from the price this green line was really important. People were selling it and that's why the price could not be exceeded. And if they move further you see the same thing happening again and again and again. Now as you can see this is a double talk and I'll try to double it up.

You hear prices fall. So if I presume that's to be what I call the maxed like gain and I pick the lowest low from here and I pick the highest high as here. And lacks formatted and Dreamworks childlike and I don't want to extend the line for the previous ones. What I see you see again the levels. Now at this low level this red line was at an extreme level. The price never crossed up but it was taking support on this green line. See it's within these two lines now although Fibonacci level to this one that we have made is for a limited period of time but the price is following it. If I move further the price still follows it and it breaks up like this line. And now the slide act has the support see it supported it went up and now will be touching the crane 9 and discrimination act of support.

So this is how people get to know they like Target. You would be seeing on social media or on TV people are telling you that they expect the price to reach X target. You'll be seeing research of different brokers like you search companies and they will be giving you a specific target. So this question always comes into mind : how the hell do they know? Coggins who provides them to target. How do they get to know those tactics? What makes them sure that these targets will be hit? Now I'm showing you and I have gone from here. OK so the rest of the period was not considered this fall but still from a note you automatically can click here loads and don't say were so strong that it stopped to like tries here. Fell off and put support on the scene green line that Fibonacci retracement has made again like rose up by his support and again met the resistance right here the red line then again fell off green supporting then again rose back up.

And if you look at it it's getting all the support and resistance, see it stopped at the scene break like how come it always stops at the same red light at the scene like that Fibonacci to Christmas is like. And the answer lies in the percentages that it's providing now Fibonacci. The person who made these non-birds displacement pushing made them not liked in the last century. He made many many years ago many many centuries ago. So he did a complete learning. I've read different books and they tell that he took this strategy from the Urbik scholars and brought them into Europe and so on and so forth. But the point is that these loans work. Now what are these limits? That's a brilliant question now from this bottom kill list up the top number is zero percent.

Then comes twenty two point six percent because 0.26. If you multiply by 100 percent you'll get the percentage for just twenty point six percent. Then comes eight point two percent full. Then comes 50 percent for then comes sixty one point eight percent fall. Then come. I cannot see it. We don't. And comes seventy eight point six percent fall and then come 100 percent full. So you can see these different percentages are false and they are extremely powerful. As you can see I have made this as a shorter term Cringle. And this is a longer term trend line because the higher and the lower and higher the higher the lines are. And they give you a higher target.

Now how do you know when the previous Fibonacci lines are irrelevant and you deform on your one whenever the price crosses this hundred percent level is zero. Well then you make and you were people not doing Christmas and now this is the last you know this is the highest time. So we didn't—the price will and here. OK so you can see the price you know and it looks like a bang. All those lows. See that's just slow and stop.

Why not just drop it? It could stop here. No. That's the power of these numbers. It makes them stop at the exact level and even if it crosses below and comes back up on the line then you want to give you a target now. OK. This target could be achieved. Now you're reading on the basis of Fibonacci.

You don't like to play straight. Exactly. Basically you know that 1:06 crossing this line of quantitate really the next line is at 24 nine thousand six hundred seven. Eighty six hundred eighty six. But you're right the traders in the hedge fund community don't bet on the old one already. He said there is a famous saying that to you as an investor don't eat the last penny which means the $1 incident is not like eating what you should eat. Wonder if he had 1.40 cents because the price was before that. Why? Because once everyone puts the selling at the same line then the investor who is buying is going to think that he may not be able to sell himself on the line to the South before the time. And that's how the price Dunch below line. So he went below. But then it fell off and on the line people started to buy Kroes up.

That's the power of Fibonacci lines and if you look at it it's crossing up, falling off and opening higher. Now when we open higher above all, the Mark above our highest high number is gone. It's not worth it. And the producer number we extend those lines. And it tells us that this line is crossed. So you can see a higher line, see the highest line and stop at the same line. Now if you remember this was May 2012 and this was August 2012. It's like 2012 and now what we're trading in is 2013. Next an impact from this low but still the lake levels are working completely. Now let me show you another thing because you move to extend lines and let's pick Fibonacci retracement and make it from deathblow this I OK and then you go here. Sorry. No you don't do that.

Basically you pick people to try to respond to a cane and you pick this high that this low. Now let me show you one more thing. I'm just making the chalk smaller. OK. And looming out. Now the thing that I wanted to show you is if you can see the doctor line on my mouse that off the 45 and here 6:48 the next level it gives us 58. So the gap becomes far larger when it really causes that. And as you have seen you can balance them. So there is a huge difference. But now the question comes up: how do you know what makes these levels so special? Dr. lies again in percentages. Sixty one point eight percent. So with a 100 percent mark. That is the highest high. It crosses up then it goes 261 then goes to six to 1.8 then it goes to sixty one point eight. Then it goes to four hundred and twenty point six percent.

So the gaps in the root cause of the high become extremely larger. Now if you look at it right here you have the smaller gaps. The biggest is on the lake below the low and above the highest pie percent. The price certainly jumped from 45 03 till 61 97. That's huge. That's $17 in profit and it's not only 17. That's approximately a 40 percent rise. And if you look at it that's 100 percent gain x hundred sixty one point eight percent gain. So it's poker, not 40 percent. Sixty one point eight percent gain about-I and that's how you see on TV the detailing. Once the price of that 45 Hicklin Goggles six. How the hell do you know now not on it like. And what he'd be telling you 1:54 don't pull it off for 60 because they themselves know that will Gurukul sixty one point ninety seven so they won't tell you the same thing.

They'll be rounding it off so that it makes the number for themself. And no one can prove it. Back to food and notchy back whenever you ask Harbi to come up with these numbers. I give you a fundamental reason or that tells you that they came up by himself but to conclude fundamentals you have to click like you have to get a lot of data and phone e-tailing was not possible. But if you just look at it right here it's giving you the percentages without any data required because it's. The historic person stages the historic formula. The formula that still works I'm sure right now and it still works. The price stops at the same level. Now I'm extending the lines here.

And let's zoom in to see what happens next. And at it the price moved here. It went straight straight straight to the job higher above the highs and went beyond the high. The first line and now it's crossing. Now for this crossing here what do we expect? That's the number one question. Now off to the first high off like this line 28 55. The next it comes to four dollars. I can see the line. It's 48-29. Forty dollars. Twenty nine cents. And if they move forward to show you a crisis crossing now you can easily say that 48 and it did cost it. Now once it's crossing the next guy comes to this line for I'm 58 so you can tell your friends easily that you can expect to go to 58 now although it's not going up but it's like roaming around alliance. So once it broke this red line you can either tell your friends that things have changed and it can go to TA-DA tasty.

And if it crosses this target it can go to this target. And if you have heard any of these hotel listings you tell the same thing and you always get amazed how come they know that and just look at it, stop at the same line and go for that. How do you tell an investor doesn't know the game plan but the player sure does. And he is not using a rocket science technique. He's using the same normal technique. But only he knows that he isn't doing anything extra. He's just picking an indicator that works for centuries. Just look at it, it's now crossing the PSII of 64. So this is how people begin to make good will definitely get it. Now if they get none of this and extend the previous four lines. You cross 45. You were all believing it to be going to 62 and it did.

And now after sixty two you are already considering 89 940 and for just zoomin because it's really small and some of you might not be able to see it. So now if you look at the price that rises up. Now you have no raw data, you have no information on flying off Facebook. You have no financial analysis or fundamental data but still you have an idea what will happen if it crosses above or lower. Now it has crossed the line. So now your aim becomes this fine or if it crosses the line up then your aim becomes just like a simple trick. That's what you always hear from the market research analyst. And what are they doing? Yeah. Picking the steam indicator again and again. And just look at it. It's below that. So if you ask anybody like a research analyst they'll be telling you all now good days it's not all word X Y Z problems.

It goes above the line like I still would be telling you now they expect the price to go up to around 90. And just look at it the price is rising up slowly and gradually although this takes many many years. But the point is how do people come up with Doggett's This is how they come up with the gothic. Now the prices within these two are bent so this is a team that will still know it's going straight straight straight. But both this 1:54 long line and let's move straight going straight straight straight straight straight straight x. Move forward. And now it's about to charge $90. Now if you remember initially I told you that usually don't expect the full number. This is 90 Naba because everyone is already selling it at 89. There are eighty-nine toady's that line.

So 89 could be achieved by die's point here is 86. So let's look for that now right here. Just look at it, it does it now. It took many many months. But the question remains once it crossed here in 2014 may it Doc around one year in one month 30 months and preached reached the. And if it crosses this line it will reach this line 160. So you can hear people say right here that OK now they expect the price to rise up. And if you just look at it it does take but it's still lower than the like. It's still within these two lines. So people when we see each day like if you heard retail investors will be saying the price only touched a previous high treason because they know if it costs to produce high then a new low will come in.

Otherwise these are hosed to the price of stocking. And if you look at it to support at the same level it fell off but then came back above . So this is how you view yourself as an get in the truck and also make Tagaq nowadays are not short term targets. These are long term targets but they are targets. They help you understand what the price is doing. If the price falls from this line then this target is really achievable. And the difference between them is huge. This is 88 89 and this is 62. That's what we should do. How do you do? $17 that's 30 percent. In between these two lines and that's how the media players know stuff that you don't know because they have some targets in their mind so they're creating become so much easier than a retail investor who doesn't know anything. Become so critical because he is black. That's why I'm teaching them because I have made money and I believe you can also make money with it. Use the said focus on it. Thank you.

Demo Account

Hi guys. Today I'll help you understand how to make a free demo trading account. Now I dot.com AIG is a company that is good in terms of a broker. Now I'm not saying to open an account with them. The real account you can open with any broker you like but for a demo account I'm just giving you a demonstration to make a demo. You need to enter a username password. Name surname if you like. Country main contact number. Even address and try our demo and your Demo conference. We meet once you have made it and applied the strategy discussed in this Book. At least apply the strategy for six months. Open an Excel sheet to see if you can make money. Open a diary. Write down what are your mistakes. Because usually you need some time to come into the groove of investing. Once you have invested six months or let's say twelve months in a demo account go for a real account in the real account invest as little as you can and then for six months.

Make sure that that little amount grows. I'm just giving an example. If you have invested a hundred dollars. Make sure that you grow it. Two hundred and twenty dollars. Even when you grow up a foreigner and 20 dollars don't stop. Wait. Trade the same thing for six months at least you can trade for a year or so but trade for at least six months. Once you've done that then invest more money. Otherwise don't go from the stock with the heavy amount. First learn. Now what do they mean by loan? When you were in school you were doing the scene mat or theme strategy to be applied again and again so that in the real exam in the final exam you remember that strategy. The same thing applies in investing.

You need to test their strategy again and again so that once you are investing the real amount the heavy amount you are sure that you will go straight to you by heart and to do that you need to invest six months in a demo account where no real money is involved and then six months with a shoestring budget in a real account. That's why you would like to completely transform. That's how you will completely transform. The point is to invest six months each in total. You're in demo and real account and then move to heavy about once you have done that. I am sure then you will become a professional figure. Thank you.

VIX

Hi guys today we will discuss the VIX Index. Now in this book we want to be following the VIX index. But what I am trying to tell you is a learning phase which will help you really to ward off problems because basically when you are creating There are many things involved. The strategy that we discussed in this Book will help you make good short selling decisions but you need to look for other variables that come from your trading insight because at the end of the day you need to be sure that you're on the right track. Now the plan can help you make money but you have to know what's really happening in the market now to know what it's happening in the market. The best thing is the index.

One of the top most like things tech work in the market because there are many things in the market that don't work. This doesn't help you but VIX is not one of them. This is something that really helps. Now if you look at it if you are gaining stocks then you can see they are different VIX Index CVO the S&P 500. This is an inverse trick which you discuss in the next chapter. You have got dynamic VX shut down futures weekly futures mid-tone futures if you just zoom down. Medium term linked to S 500 linked to SPF chaulk down linctus be 500 beat up 500 futures and so on and so forth. Even you can see that there is a company named when comped and which vexed in Hanoi Vietnam I guess. So you can see this is really popular. There are many many indexes available and if returned to CBOE VIX index which will come within a minute.

Then I can explain to you what really happens now. I will tell you that if you're trading in S&P do they keep an eye on the VIX index. You have to know what is happening in the market. Now you might say OK I'm trading in gold. And why should I look at the S & P 500 now? Basically our trading plan doesn't affect getting vex. So you have no problem at all. Number one. Number two even though you have no problem still you sure have an eye on it because if things go down then you have to be vigilant. Have to be on the Guard because sometimes as we have discussed in Lake later on in the Book in the example sometimes the strategy changes so quickly that you have to be on the Guard because. Even in the normal stances the strategy happens to give you like a day notice max one day notice. Today's trading day has ended. So from 4:00 p.m.

to Lactaid tonight at 11:00 p.m. Then you will sleep and the next morning market will shock. So what do you have? Five six hours. So you have to be on your toes. You have to follow the plan and look for other signs that conform to your plan. And one of the signs is the CBOE water quality index. Now how does the VIX Index look? Number one index looks when he reaches the highest point. It means people are fearful that a fall will come in when it reaches the lower part of the VIX index like say here people believe while it is not that much problematic. Basically how does VIX get critics ? They just don't do monthly, basically extending itself from buy and sell orders in options. Now if I am fearful then Perico or my risk I'll be buying options so that if default comes in I can save money.

Now what do I mean by that. Let me explain. Institutional investors hedge fund managers aren't all the big fish to people whom we call big fish, the people who invest a million shares. Now if I need to sell those million shares then I can't because in a day it's not enough for me to sell cosmoline shares there are too many variables involved that may not help me out. The market can crash the stocks that I hold if I'm going to sell them quickly. The stock price can crash and that can lead me to huge losses. So I cannot tell within a day's notice. The plan that we discussed in this book is based on short term trading because most of my students are really getting whiskers. But if I need to sell I can't. So what do I do now? If Let's presume I boarded here, I could have reached here. Right. What should I do?

How do I get out? I still sell options strategies to reason because it tells me at. I can offload them at a later date but I can sell those options at the highest price near the highest price so that is one strategy and does like Index follow stock. Now if you look at it what is the date below mentioned will be dated This is September 2008. Everyone was fearful. Just look at it till 2014. It fell off but the people were extremely afraid here. Let's go back to 1998 August. People are fearful. Is it the fall? So you could see it tells you when people are fearful. Now I'm not saying to completely follow it. No I'm not saying that but I'm saying do look and I own it when the people are more fearful when I deal make available to buy because if you look at it here it's at the extreme no so people are willing to buy it right now.

Let's move to some other VIX S&P 500 index or to go there for a two minute wait a minute. Let me turn today into our next KOO-KOO mentally I look at it mentally. People became more fearful in October 2008. Just look at it to fix it at the highest point. This is the monthly chart not something like what law chalked up. This is the longest dump possible. If you look at it in October it reached the highest point in November. The EU went higher at the last bite. Look at the spike and now it has just reached a pre-2007 level 2006 December low which makes it that everyone believes that the market will rise up from today onward. 2018 is court. Why? Because it's his job to look at it. Let's move to S and P A. Let me put a new one S and P 500 likely to show you something. Let it be now this is a CFT but it usually follows the index or you can find the index.

Wait a minute please. Let's follow this for a minute. If we make it, we make monthly room Teutons. Now we discussed 2008 he committed St. Beefeaters. Just give me a minute Boom-Boom right now a thing to note right here people were most fearful. Now let me give you an insight from the institutional investor point of view. I won't care. The people are most likely featureful. I know that's the point. Fall. If you look at it this is October 2008 and if I go to the chart this is October to talk. Now if you look at it here it did fall for the next four months. Right. This month is November. It spiked you in for the. So I don't believe it as a sign of complete failure. Now I'm talking about the monthly low and I'm not talking about the daily level right now.

So look for them on two levels. First it will tell you what is happening on the monthly level. It doesn't mean that it's dangerous. It means for institutional investors that. OK. Now like could stop because if everyone is bullish and this means things are not that bad just look at it to 2000 low in September. Let's look at it here. Two thousand eleven September the extreme fall. People are fearful right here in this fall. They were fearful right. So on the monthly level you can kind of reverse. Now if you look at it here in 2006 it's November when everyone would like some kind of her bullish 2006 late 2006 what October November 2006. It was not like it was not something to be bullish on. If you look at it once everyone sees it OK. People are fearful of Nordyke.

They only made this rally and then they started to put stocks on the people. If you look at it in the fall the first hit on this record mark on this red line in 2005 February on the Fall 2005 February data was very. People would have walked into the restroom not in the second mark because till that time they had made the price right. They have made the index rise from 12 below until sorry 11 81 till 4300. That's a that percent rise index you could rise to 30-50 percent max. They don't cry 300 percent. So you can see that they have made a lot of money and that's why I always tell my students to look for the monthly first to analyze, then a reversal can happen. Because if everyone is fearful in any solution investor won't be that fearful he will be fearful first then others.

If I'd just done the VIX index from Motley to daily and then we just move out to two 2000 eight Why don't they let Disko go to monthly daily. They don't let us do that. But no problem. Lex GITTOES of this is 2011 right. Yup 2011 September to go to daily and 2008 September is on target now have go now just to show you one more time takes you out. Zoom out zoom in. So don't get it in the middle. Ghettos in the low end right here. This is the top right. Zoom out and make it dash and wow. You can see the 2000 11 in the first fall from here. 2010 may kill 2000 in January. No fap for starting 2011. February starts just look at it here right on this rice. People were becoming less fearful. Three from the top. They will feel full right here. It is 2010 may mean being in. So that you can clearly see it.

Yep. Right. People will feel like they're fooling me. Two thousand ten. If I go here May 2010 may 2010 right here. People are extremely fearful. On the far right here. So they started to sell. But as an investor I wouldn't be afraid I would look at it as a buying opportunity. And that's exactly what happens. From August 2010 to April 2011 it cruises from August 2010. July August right here. Just look at it from August 2010. People were less fearful; they were buying, buying , buying , buying. Now this is the first fall. This forced fall is December 20th. Let's look at it here. December right here people became not that fearful they were like happy Dubai because 5:59 is at Dillo. People are happy to buy one ticket at too high a price. People want to sell and get out. Right. So here people were OK OK.

They will buy it. They will not get it for the next time when the market rules. If you look at it December 28 January 14th one went Fabricant two months March April 14 four months. Now in this format the retail investor was buying to not take a break. It was a Lewis point just too much for you. This was the lowest point in those areas because markets like the rise and fall in the future were there. If I just make it tactfully you're right. People could not see in the future. Right. So right here it was at the extreme low. This was extremely low. 2010 April. And that's exactly what it is here in April 2011. It's at the same rate as the VIX index. So no one is fearful. But if you look at the S&P It was reaching the top. This is May and this second is October 2010 and if you look at it from here it's April.

And just look at it in the future. Now you can see the month on the lower part of June and July. So once people were like we're happy to buy. The market has already reached the top and it's started. If you look at it and then it started to rise in August 2011 in June July August in August if I just zoom in to show you further down here in August the first four that come in and now the second DR-DOS coming in. And in that time you could see the rising expose a Dickstein point. Now this is all July and August. Let me show footer C in September across even higher in September October so the higher end if you look at it when everyone is like thinking OK they will buy. There was not much money to be made. In the last rally till October Rick started to rise.

So you can see that the fearfulness at the extreme last moment right is up but you cannot expect it to rise up to 1000 and watch for one month in advance or even 10 days in it once it rises up at the extreme time. And if you look at it once it crossed this me you're high right to this was August 4. And if I look at here this was August in the fall the VIX started to rise on the first trial and then the price was up. And Ed this extreme point in October. Let's see what happened. Here we go. This is the October part. See October. This is October 14th. This is October 28. So you can see Netflix has come down a bit but the feel for less is if I just zoom out near the extreme point this is the extreme point previously an X is about at the same time about at the same level and then starts to drop.

See that's what I'm telling you on the scale. It held steady getting rest on our own. Because it tells though like to begin with a big fish that it's time to buy. If everyone is fearful because basically the major investor is a contrarian investor he will be buying when everyone is fearful. As Warren Buffett says it's but if you look at it on the daily mark it told you that it was dangerous right here. But one thing I bought was not that good. That's what I was trying to tell you. If you want to learn for weeks , this is the lecture I told you once. Once it fell off to the extreme lows, then the price started to rise on the first low. But did it like it grows on the lows but once it reached the top it started to rise but don't like to fall into the trap at once because each tick up right here you would be selling the stock.

No once you see it is getting the extreme hype moment then you have to be vigilant because you know now the extreme fall comes in and that's what I'm trying to tell you right here. Once the VIX read the highest point in October the false started down. Extremely faulty. Just look at it. This is 15-49. And this is 735 Datchet. 100 percent fall from 735. This is the 100 percent 15:14 from 15:14 and this is a 50 percent fall. That's my point, Civic's told you what is about to happen. Now once you learn further down you'll see sometimes you will jump in early. Our plan will give us signals to sell early somewhere around here somewhere around here somewhere around here not here. This is the first time we usually don't give the signal there.

This is the second. So it will be giving signals in the second automatize. But as you will see further it's usually not like last making trade. It's usually a small profit. This is all to fall back from here the fall is usually chop. So you can look at the mix to understand when the shop fault was coming. So you can time your trade accordingly. And that's the really important part. So VIX can help you understand a feature and if you look at all the indexes usually to follow each other they may not follow at the fall like if S&P had fallen 50 percent in this area. As we discussed just now. So Nasdaq might have fallen 30 percent. Dow might have fallen 10 percent but the fall in on all those late index even if there is no fall then it won't be rising 10 percent. It will be flat. So it's really helpful for you to learn the VIX Index because it can change the money making tanks for you. You can earn more. Thank you.

Support, Resistance & Trendlines

Hi guys today who will discuss trend lines and support and resistance sites. Now these are the most important aspects of creating because you have to understand what really is happening. And DEC will make or break the game. Now if you look at it I've not set any indicator. No baby no RVY but I'll be first focusing on supporting Andrews just like now. This is the current chalk. This is January 2018 and if you look at it I've just made lines on the highest point. Now let's look at this highest point. This is your highest point. But once you open higher it to support the high point example it closes below it. But the next day it opened above it and closed below it the next week. Same thing. It went lower than the current high and took support on the line. Now you made the line on this high. We knew and you didn't like we will be following it. We don't know that.

Right you have made the line on the talk. This is too low. Even here it's not touching the line but it's staying above the line. Now this is the power of support and resistance because once you are trading you have to have an understanding. OK. If it falls, what can I expect? Example another example. Let me make a line right here on this low. No one will take me. So it went higher. I looked up when I made a loss. But you knew from this high that this was a second line. If I make a third line on many clothes on this number if you look at it this one two three. This is a high for my fifth close sixth open seven times seven times a dashed line. And here as well. Eight nine ten and here. Eleven went to dust 11 times and went higher. So after the fall we knew that it can reach this line or this line which is this low or this high. As simple as that.

And if you look at it, it makes it take acting. So you have to have an understanding of what is dummy. And it is a daily chart. If your doctor gets a monthly chalk things change, come Blackley. Now this high is here. Wait a minute. Yeah. This Iowas this line and decided to test it. And this is a major supporter. All right. Now I have fallen on this open on this high line. So if an apple falls from here first we just put a little bit in this. Now let me zoom out to see if there are any further options. No they are not. Now let me make it. More important is to cite examples on the monthly scale I'm making on the tree like opening close here. If you look at it, it grows up. This was especially old Boothill and 12 September park Denslow. The flash crash 2015 it went the same no how on it it went the same low yes it went for park from this like line.

People would be like Major with troops leaving by buying it because they knew if it is falling so quickly it can come back up. And this was a major support level. That's what took him Day four. You have to understand what really is happening because if you're trading something Dan you should have major support in your mind because right here it was a resistance. It stopped here and went for but then you cranked up and it became a support line like Frank Lawler back from this line buying gaming buying came in and again buying gaming and it stopped here and again buying gaming. And it made higher highs. So once you let's presume you Bodek some. Are you shocked that they're here then how will you know what we'll be doing? To me, your support level. You were shocked and told them the market is certainly true. It certainly is.

Crocodile but at that moment you need to ask yourself we cannot like go from non-Intel hunting down to $10. No it can't. So what could be the major profit you undertake? And if that idea is being achieved and that's the best thing you're getting the money because at the end of the day you're taking the scoresheet to make money. And if it falls and it can give you what your desired Pondexter best thing you simply squared off and wait for the next short selling opportunity. As simple as that. No problem. That is the game plan. This is a monthly skill that I've shown you. No problems at all now let us go to Citibank. Here we go. Citigroup exploding. Wait a minute. So my basic point is support and resistance really work. They are a powerhouse now in Citigroup. The same thing will repeat. Now let me pick any date.

Oh let's pick this one. Just look at it here. It closed up and fell off right. So now I will be just pulling up only the top numbers, example this high. Dan I'm picking this high down. I am picking this high and then I'm picking Dessa. So these are all the highs now just look at it. Just let me do my best. I picked only these highs. It crossed up, made a low on the same high, went up meter high on the same high rental or made time flow on the same low. Their entire media high around the same high rank low may get low around the same low. And even this low in the low. And what's it like to get around on that high level and what's your cost? Boom it's going up. See. So. Anyone.

Like if you want to understand the long term effect you can see these highs once like it came back from the low to reach back up on the high. It does seem high. Again and again and again just look at this. And another one right here. This is the second high I've just baked this last line. Like assuming what really happened at that line. If you look at it, let me zoom in again to show you the basic difference. Now although once we had like zoomed out and we were looking at a thing with no major impact. But if you look at it, it is closed above the line. And the next day on Sunday below that line. How strange. He closed up but opened Willow just to honor that line. And the next day it opened up on the line and it went up and down again , dashed this line and opened your fee on the exact line it was doing the thing. Just honoring them.

That's what the power of these lines are currently. They have not put blinds on every like number but if you look at it you will understand that it does play out. It makes sense just to follow them and it will give you a real insight. Just look at this. I've put this line on just low on Denslow and it stopped at that high at that line. And when Keilor just looked at it I found another line on these two loads. Right you just keep clicking. The first try was docked on the line. Second prize was also stopped in their line and fell off. Doug Rawhi continued to go up but then dipped for the second nine and so on and so forth. But the main point is that it stopped at the same high point.

That is why I always tell you to look for these lines that will change the day. It is really really important because they are the ones that helped you understand what to do and what not to do. Therefore my aim remains the same for all my might. I always look for these little things because they've really ironed out the problems that are the best things they hope you understand. OK. If this high cost high design went lower then these are Dellec problems. And let's look at it in this way. He committed too slowly. Right. OK. Yeah. Just low and slow. Right now my point is that it has reached a high point. Right. And then. Now if you look at it closely you'll find that once it hits it is just like lying to major like distance to cover with this line.

So from this low Tony 7:38 or take 668 play major players knew 45 was achievable. So that means $17 back means 50 percent gain from 36. That's huge. Now Turkomen are you dealing with her it's like he's blind he cannot see this but a major investor wants this fall will happen. We know it all OK. No problem. We can make some money and take you back and they will be jumping in and then you will be like you are there still will be shocked you'll be saying how on earth day you will come back. Just look at this. I've now changed to Khelil. And what do you see? The theme lines happen to make sense and just look at it here. I made the line on the extreme low right. Yes. June 2013 it touched 2014 April as well and this line was formed on this lows. Are these lows? It does the low gain.

Now I was formed on this high and it stopped after some look just looking at the difference. This is December 2014 and this is June 2015. That's a six month difference. It still stops at the same level. How on earth. Just look at it. If literally you didn't know what was ahead. You just formed a line on this low. This is below. This is below. Now if the eighth 2014 April just moves ahead. And what do you see? It fell off and took refuge around the team low fi. This was the second blow because this was the first low. This should be the second lowest. Why? Because this is the low first. This is the open close second. And then you have this open third open for this open fifth open six. So it's like five or six times it does it. So this was a second important line and under Vitullo it just scored from this line. If a change to the Deely mark and if I just move ahead.

No, this is made of all the lines in Castlemilk Sumach. We made all the lines based on 2015. Just look at it here. 2014 2015 and once you go to 2000 like Reekie level our lines made sense in 2015 Athill in 2013 July of El just Luketic our lines meet fans of free Ty and it's not like you mean Playchess time kind of thing. It's just common sense. It makes those lines and if you just do our plex zoom out farther down right. Just look at it this height. All of it seems like these two Heiss seem like this is the line that we draw in 2015. But it was touching the heights right here. Just look at them. It makes sense. Hi Don. The same line this high was near that same line. Although we won't come this high. But my point is even if you like to move quickly back you will see all those lines telling you to trust gay work.

So if you are trading just look at those lights. They will help you understand OK if the data is just low and low could be dashed. So you can expect a major change. Now remember Citigroup this is the monthly chart. All those levels. Mark Dasht here sees that is what makes sense. This is 1994. So they made sense. And once the price went higher at DEC time like the point offer, it was a well stocked day for it could go even higher because there was no major resistance. But one text has fallen lower now the major problems have started to come up again and that's why it's a make or break stuff.

Any stock that you see if it gets crossed all the media like problems like it. In 93 it may decide to go but once it crossed this high of 81 it was boom boom boom. It went from one pill 360. That's what it took huge twenty four thirty two decks four and a half times they're done with that one. This is October 1995 and this is June 1998. So let's presume two years and 10 months max. And if you go to this first high that is what two years and it takes what x. So what they didn't do and a half years you make four and a half 400 and 50 percent are going simple.

And this is a good stock. So you would be earning David. And those are separate. This is only by Intel profit. No David except cash to it. And you make so much money that that is why I always tell you to look at things from a different perspective. And once you look at them the losses that have gone out of the window only the profit they make or break you you will be in. So that oh God I've missed Citibank Citigroup before and 50 percent profit. I bought some other company which gave me 250 percent profit. But still you are in profit. Why? Because you have equipped yourself with the best techniques that major investors use and you can not even know about it. Dax what matters. Thank you.

www.ingramcontent.com/pod-product-compliance
Lightning Source LLC
Chambersburg PA
CBHW071930210526
45479CB00002B/617